THE ROYAL
HORTICULTURAL
SOCIETY

the
HALF
HOUR
ALLOTMENT

THE ROYAL
HORTICULTURAL
SOCIETY

the
HALF
H⊙UR
ALLOTMENT

LIA LEENDERTZ

Consultant Will Sibley

F

FRANCES LINCOLN LIMITED
PUBLISHERS

To Rowan

Frances Lincoln Ltd
4 Torriano Mews
Torriano Avenue
London NW5 2RZ
www.franceslincoln.com

A catalogue record for this book is
available from the British Library.

ISBN 13: 978-0-7112-2605-0
ISBN 10: 0-7112-2605-9
Printed and bound in Singapore

1 2 3 4 5 6 7 8 9

CONTENTS

1 The half-hour principle 6

2 Taking on a plot 16

3 Deciding what to grow 30

4 Growing the right amount of the best varieties 44

5 Planning the first year 74

6 Nurturing your plants 88

7 Keeping on top of your plot 104

8 Managing pests and diseases 118

9 Some optional extras 130

10 What next? 144

Further reading 156

Some mail order suppliers 156

Index 158

Acknowledgments 160

1

THE HALF-HOUR PRINCIPLE

Everyone wants an allotment these days, and quite right too. Not only is having an allotment a fantastic way to get exercise and fresh air, but it means that you can have complete control of the food that comes into your home. Food scares are a constant concern and the idea of seeing your food through from plot to plate appeals to many people. The rise in the popularity of allotments is a direct and understandable response to concerns about pesticide residues on fruit and vegetables and a lack of trust in the large corporations that supply most of our food. We may also be aware that flying our beans over from Kenya or apples from South Africa does not help the environment. We know that food tastes best when fresh, and that supermarket produce is most likely picked a good few days before it reaches us. Some people realize that the varieties that supermarkets encourage farmers to grow are chosen more often for their ability to withstand the extreme conditions of packing and transporting procedures than they are for taste, and we want to be reminded what real tomatoes and strawberries taste like. Allotments seem a perfect solution to all these worries. They are local, environmentally friendly and hand back control of food production to the cook and the consumer, by enabling you to grow your own delicious fresh fruit and vegetables. The only food miles involved are as often as not those they travel on the back of a bicycle.

But so often things go wrong. If you've tried having an allotment before, perhaps you know the story: you get your plot and set about it with gusto, throwing all your spare time into it. After a few weekends of exhaustion and backache friends start leaving messages wondering what has happened to you, and it suddenly occurs to you that you have been neglecting a few things around the house – DIY, pets, children – and so you miss a week, and then another. By the time you get back to your plot the perennial weeds have started to creep back, a fresh crop of annual weeds has sprouted, and the areas you had meticulously cleared on those first keen Sundays are starting to look, well, much as they did when you started. The rot sets in, and your prized plot soon becomes a source of worry and guilt, assuaged only vaguely by the occasional frenzied weekend visit, rather than the gloriously bountiful spot you had imagined. Sooner or later a firm but fair letter from the allotment committee arrives, asking you to maintain your plot to a higher standard or consider giving it up. You haven't the heart to struggle any more, and bow to the inevitable.

Despite the fact that allotments have never been so popular and many even have long waiting lists, a large number of newly adopted plots are abandoned within the year. This is disheartening for allotment committees, but is arguably worse for the poor would-be allotmenteer, left with nothing but a sense of failure and a trapped nerve.

RIGHT By following the half-hour principle you can have a well-managed plot like this with the minimum amount of effort

NEXT PAGE Tending an allotment can boost health and happiness as well as allowing you to produce delicious food

THE HALF-HOUR PRINCIPLE

The half-hour allotment principle outlined in this book was dreamt up by Will Sibley, a nurseryman and allotment holder. Despite the fact that he is constantly on the go, with a more-than-full-time job, making regular trips abroad and having fingers in multiple pies, his plot is well ordered and perfectly manicured, and meets a good proportion of his and his family's fruit and vegetable needs. He has worked out a way to maintain this vision of productivity on half an hour's work a day, with weekends off. The aim of this book is to tap into this system and show other allotmenteers how to do the same.

Will saw that most new allotmenteers take as their role models those good old boys who spend at least half their lives on their plot. We sigh: 'They are so generous with their huge crops of beans', or 'How do they manage three plots?' before throwing ourselves into trying to mimic them. What we fail to see is that for these people their allotment is a way of life. They choose to allow their allotment plot to take up their entire lives, but it is entirely unnecessary for its effective maintenance. They do so because they like it. It may well be essential to their social life, but those of us who cannot put in the same amount of time should certainly not feel inferior. The reality is that when they arrive each day they stand around and have a chat with their next door neighbour, stroll around the plot scratching their chins for a bit, before having a nice cup of tea and

considering their day's tasks. Hours are wasted. The only reason their plots look so good is because they would look utterly ridiculous if they didn't manage to keep their plots looking half decent.

Will would not call himself a keen gardener so much as a keen eater. He came up with his system because he likes eating good, fresh food, but he didn't want to give up half his life and all his leisure time in order to get it. Not only is he as busy – work- and family-wise – as anybody else on his allotment site, but he also has other things to do with his spare time when he is not working, such as 'fishing on a fast flowing trout stream or drinking a good bottle of wine while listening to jazz'. He had also become depressed by meeting new allotmenteers – people similar to him, with jobs and families, and with similar reasons for having an allotment – and seeing them struggle to keep up with the old boys, and watch their enthusiasm and interest wane and eventually disappear.

Will's experience as a nurseryman gave him the knowledge to do the right things at the right times, and to work with the soil and the seasons, and he knew that doing so makes it so much easier to get what you want out of a plot. So he set himself various parameters, and went about devising a system that would work for him, and could also be easily translated to other plots by people like him: people who do not have the time or the inclination to spend days endlessly pottering, but who like to eat delicious, fresh vegetables.

He was not hugely ambitious about the amount of produce he should expect, but thought that there should be a basic minimum return for his investment. The rules went as follows: he would work on the allotment for a maximum of two and a half hours a week, and the allotment would provide a salad for his family every day of the year and some other green vegetable every day of the year. If you have visions of bountifully handing out mounds of gourmet veg to your friends and family this may sound a bit mean, although of course there will be times when there is an awful lot more. On the other hand, if you have struggled with gluts and famines in the past this may sound wonderful to you – all that you would expect. You may appreciate how tricky it is to get a constant supply of vegetables all year round, and just how fantastically welcome a plateful of something fresh is in the depths of winter. At its most basic level, this is the promise of the half-hour system: it means that as long as you put in the time you will never be without at least some of your own fresh vegetables and salads.

So how do you put the system into practice? First and foremost the half-hour principle is about persistence. The best way to keep on top of all the many jobs that need carrying out at your allotment is to be there regularly. You will need to spend two and a half hours every week at your plot to put this system into practice properly, but this time is really best divided into five half-hour visits, one on each weekday, or, if that is not possible, into two hour-and-a-quarter visits over

two days, perhaps at the weekend. Two and a half hours of digging would strain the back of a navvy, but most people can just about manage half an hour. Regular, daily visits also keep you wonderfully in touch with your plot – and this is where you can learn from the old boys: a constant, vigilant presence will help you spot when things need watering, when pests are attacking and the exact moment when crops have reached their peak.

Secondly it is about organization. So many people arrive on their plots and just wander around for ten minutes – that's a third of your daily time allowance; then they flit from job to job with no real plan or system. Ideally you should spend a few minutes at the end of each visit planning your next, but if that is too far a stretch, make a quick tour of the allotment when you first arrive, plan your work in your mind and then get straight down to it. Even better is to break your half hour down into ten-minute chunks – you might measure out 1 sq m (10 sq ft) of soil that needs digging over, sow a small row of carrots and then hoe the weeds under your gooseberry bushes. It doesn't matter that there is still 29 sq m (310 sq ft) of soil to dig, that you haven't sown your lettuces and that weeds are springing up under your apple tree and loganberries: you'll be back tomorrow, and the next day. Quickly this way of thinking will become second nature.

An important part of this system is to grow what you need, rather than suffering the tyranny of gluts and famine. You may be impressed in your first year when fellow allotment holders start handing out carrier bags full of spinach and courgettes, but you will soon come to realize that almost no one wants courgettes at the height of summer. Everyone but the new kid on the block is sick of the sight of them and has probably spent the best part of the last two weeks stewing and freezing them and turning the remainder into courgette jam. There is no point in growing 3m (10ft) of French beans that all mature at the same time, sending you into a preserving frenzy, when you can grow 1m (3ft) and have exactly what you need, fresh.

Closely related is careful consideration of the types of vegetables you grow. If your aim is to grow everything your family will want to eat for the entire year, this is not the system for you: we are not talking about *Good Life*-style self-sufficiency. Although there will be times of the year when your half-hour plot will supply your entire fruit and vegetable needs, achieving this is not really the aim and you may often find yourself supplementing your grown produce with bought. The idea, though, is that you grow the more expensive, luxury items, and the ones that really

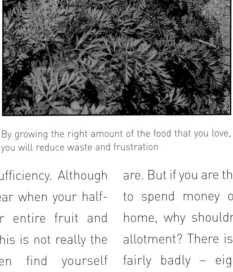

By growing the right amount of the food that you love, you will reduce waste and frustration

benefit from being eaten freshly picked. So you may find that under this system you won't grow enough onions and maincrop potatoes to store away and keep you going through the winter, but you will have all the asparagus, raspberries, properly 'new' potatoes and fresh, crispy salad leaves you can eat, plus a year-round supply of sweet, tiny carrots no thicker than your little finger. Will calls it 'dinner-party food'; it is the sort of thing that you would enjoy serving to your guests.

The final tenet is to use everything at your disposal to make life easier for yourself. There is a tradition within the allotment community of making do, recycling and, above all, keeping costs down. This is excellent and admirable, and it makes allotment sites the quirky and creative places they are. But if you are the sort of person who is happy to spend money on labour-saving devices at home, why shouldn't you do the same on the allotment? There is no need to grow – probably fairly badly – eighty times the number of seedlings you need, clogging up every windowsill in your house, when you can reach for a catalogue and order the dozen or so that you need to feed your family, already beautifully grown and ready to plant. True, such purchases could be called an unnecessary expense, but if they make your life much easier, and if that makes you less likely to throw in the towel, they're well worth it.

This book will take you through all these points in detail, and give you the knowledge you will need to put them into practice on your own plot. It provides guidance on getting started and on setting up your plot to make life easier for yourself in the long run. It will also provide work plans to help get you into the half-hour way of thinking as well as advice on growing individual vegetables, and the amounts that you need to sow and plant to provide for yourself and your family without massive gluts. There will be many tips on alternative ways of working that will help cut down on the graft.

Of course it is possible to grow vegetables not in an allotment but in your own garden. If you are fortunate enough to have the space in your own garden, you can apply the half-hour principle there. You are far more likely to pop out there and do a few minutes here and there in the morning and then again when you first get home, and so you are much more likely to keep on top of jobs such as weeding, watering, and sowing at the right times. In this way, you are likely to be able to lower the time that you need to spend caring for it to less than half an hour a day. You will have a ten-minute allotment. The equivalent of a quarter plot – about 60 sq m (650 sq ft) – should give ample space to provide plenty of fresh fruit and veg for yourself and your family; you could probably do very well with even less.

Now all this may sound a little dry to you. Perhaps you are thinking: 'What's the point of getting an allotment if I only ever get to spend half an hour up there and never have time to get to know a few people?' Perhaps you are retired, or unemployed, or just happen to have plenty of time on your hands. I certainly don't want to sound like a killjoy, and I well know that one of the major attractions of having an allotment is the quality time you spend there, chatting with and getting to know all sorts of people you would never normally have the chance to meet, while at the same time enjoying that rare commodity, fresh air. But even if you have all the time in the world at your disposal, do you really want to spend it digging and weeding? Nobody wants to make life harder for themselves than is strictly necessary and if your plot is in order you will enjoy your time there so much more. You will be able to converse with the old timers on an equal footing, without the constant worry that you are about to be told off or disapproved of. The point of this book is to give you the tools to manage your plot in the minimum amount of time and with the minimum amount of effort. Once you have put in your daily half hour, the rest of your time is your own for chatting, sunbathing, barbecuing or just sniffing the flowers. The old boys will be desperate to know your secret.

2

TAKING ON A PLOT

Setting up your plot well, right at the beginning, can make a huge difference to its long-term success. This chapter aims to show you how to get hold of a plot and make sure that it is the best of all of those available. It will also give you some guidelines on how to start planning your plot once you have it, and what features to include. If you put some time and thought into getting the basics right, it will improve the ease with which you can manage it and make you less likely to abandon it in the long run.

GETTING HOLD OF THE RIGHT PLOT

Choosing a plot with good amenities and access, and in the right kind of condition can make the difference between success and failure, so you must be prepared to be choosy. With allotments being in high demand this can be easier said than done, and it may seem that you will have to take whatever you are offered, but there are a few things you can do to push the odds in your favour.

The first step is to contact your local council. It will let you know which sites are near by and may give you a contact number for individual sites or for an area manager. Consider how near a plot is to your home. You are much more likely to be able to keep visiting an allotment regularly if you can walk to it within a fairly short time, so it may be worth going on a waiting list for one near by, rather than just taking one that is a few miles further away because it is the first thing that is available. In some parts of the country every site has a waiting list. There is nothing much you can do to speed the process up, except perhaps call the plot secretary occasionally to remind them how keen you are. Don't be too disheartened by the thought of a wait. You are not just waiting to step into 'dead man's shoes': lots of people give up plots all the time, for all sorts of reasons – some move away, some are asked to leave, and some are first-time allotmenteers who have not read this book, poor things, and find it all too much.

One of the benefits of regularly calling and nagging your plot secretary is that you will start to develop a rapport with them. This can only work in your favour. The plot secretary knows exactly which plots are likely to come up soon, and which are the best. They will probably not want to hand the prized ones over to the likes of you. Once you are established on an allotment site, you will be astonished to discover how many people have second and even third plots, and continue to accumulate them despite a lengthy waiting list. This all seems very unfair to a newbie, but if you look at it from a plot secretary's point of view it makes sense. Their job is to keep as many plots occupied and in a good state as possible. Perhaps their pal, also up for a new plot, has a good record: he already has a plot in pristine order and they see him visiting regularly. You are an unknown quantity and could, for all plot secretary knows, abandon your plot within a year, just as the last several new allotmenteers did.

There is not really any failsafe way around this. People will always help out their friends. But it is worth being aware of the dynamics and being prepared to use whatever powers you have at your disposal – lies, bribery, flirting – to try to get to see the hidden gems. Be prepared to fight your corner, and insist they show you every plot that is not occupied. You must also always ask what plots are likely to be coming up soon and make the secretary take you to see them. Consider also taking a half-plot – see page 20.

Let's suppose you have got over the initial hurdle of the waiting list, and are being shown around the plots. Of course, there is every chance that there really is just one plot available, and you will have to take it or leave it. But if you have a choice, what should you look for? First, find out where the nearest water is. Some allotment sites allow plot holders to use hosepipes, but most people will need to carry water in watering cans from some point on the hard path up to wherever it is needed on their plot. If you are small-framed or at all frail, this will become a major job, so consider the position of water in relation to your plot above almost everything else.

It is always useful to have a plot that you can drive to. Even if you are usually able to walk there, having the possibility of driving to it allows you to move tools and equipment easily when necessary, and to nip up and pick some fresh greens and new potatoes when you have people arriving for dinner in ten minutes. At some point you will need to put some organic matter such as manure on to your plot. The difference between having it delivered straight on to the plot (there is usually someone local offering this service) where you can just cover it and use it as you need it, and having to move it barrowload by barrowload across bumpy pathways can run into back-breaking hours or even days.

Although a little shade is always welcome, it is often better to be able to control shade by erecting a shade tunnel or a shelter on a sunny plot, rather than having shade forced upon you on a permanent basis. Therefore check out how much sun your plot is likely to get each day. If it slopes to the north, the soil will take longer to warm up in spring and lose warmth faster in autumn. While looking pretty, large trees can create dense areas of shade that you will struggle with, and their roots are likely to remove nutrients and water from the surrounding soil, making some areas no-go zones for vegetables.

Obviously the amount of weeds that cover an abandoned plot will make a huge difference to how soon you can get it under control and producing for you. Most plots that have been abandoned, even if only for a few months, will look pretty weedy, especially if they have been abandoned over the summer. It makes sense to look for those that have the least amount of serious weeds on them. Brambles are among the worst, as they form thickets that need to be dug out. Japanese knotweed is a particularly nasty weed, and it would be best to avoid plots that contain it. Unless you are very lucky, though, there will be some weed problem. The best scenario is a plot covered in grass, which, although a pain, will be relatively easy to control.

Finally, choose the flattest plot available. A dramatically sloping plot can look romantic, but think of all the hours of back-breaking work that you would have to put into terracing it to make it more manageable. Even a sloping plot that has already been terraced is a pain to get around, especially with heavy equipment and wheelbarrows. Sloping plots are also likely to have drainage problems (dry top, soggy bottom) that will make every planting a complicated decision requiring extra research. Plots at the bottom of a larger slope may also have extra problems with frost, which drains downhill. This can particularly affect your ability to grow some tree fruits that blossom early in the year. A gentle slope to the south, near the top of the hill, is the only good slope.

Good amenities and access can make the difference between success and failure

HOW MUCH SPACE DO YOU REALLY NEED?

Most urban gardeners are pretty space-starved. Even those town gardens considered fairly large are usually not anywhere near big enough to grow a decent amount of vegetables. Therefore it is possible to get carried away when you first get the opportunity to have an allotment. It feels very exciting and liberating suddenly to have all that space at your disposal from as little as £10 a year, or less if you are lucky.

A standard allotment plot comprises 250 sq m (2,700 sq ft). This is a hefty area for anyone to keep under control, particularly those who have never grown anything before. The sheer size of a plot can soon become daunting. It is also entirely unnecessary.

One of the most important factors in managing your plot in half an hour a day is to be realistic about the amount of space you take on, from the start, and get the right-sized plot. Many people take on huge areas and find them a constant burden, whereas when you first start out the largest you should go for is a half plot. A quarter will probably be sufficient. This makes for a truly manageable area that you will easily be able to get under control; it will be a pleasure to look after and will provide a good selection of veg. It will also give you a chance to learn how to care for and control a vegetable plot without feeling as if you've suddenly gone into large-scale farming. In fact, you may find that there is a greater selection of half plots available on your site than whole ones, and being prepared to accept one may allow you to jump the queue. Some sites even have dedicated quarter-sized 'starter plots', which are likely to have been kept in a good condition and to have been specifically set up to give new allotment holders some experience before letting them loose on a full plot. It may seem a pain to start off on one plot and then have to move to another, but taking a half plot has the advantage of giving you the chance to show your commitment and get to know people, and that can make the difference between being allocated the plot from hell and being given a decent one that has been well worked and will be easy to keep in shape. The plot secretary may well be delighted if you accept a half plot, because it will not be such a big problem for them if it all goes wrong and you end up abandoning your plot.

ALTERNATIVES TO TAKING ON A REDUCED PLOT

But perhaps you are determined to have a full plot, or perhaps there is no other option available. There are some advantages: once you have an area under control, and have the time and energy to think about expansion, there will be no need to move to a completely new plot and start from scratch, and you will already have space that is ready to plant up while you work on clearing the rest.

If you do take on a full plot, concentrate first on putting at least half 'on hold'. To go about this you will need to clear the area of weeds, and there are a couple of ways of doing this: one is to spray off the weeds on the area that you are not going to use, and the other is to dig out the weeds by hand. You then keep subsequent weeds down by excluding light with a mulch or by strimming or mowing. For more information, see page 78. The first method is quick and relatively simple and keeps the area clean of all weeds and ready to cultivate as soon you're ready to sow or plant. If you choose this route, you will need to use a product based on the chemical glyphosate, which should combat recurring weed problems, although, there are some particularly tough weeds that will not be killed with a single dose of glyphosate, and you may have to repeat the application several times.

But for many people, however, the second method is preferable, as the whole dream of having an allotment is tied up with the idea of growing organically and attaining a really pure product that has not been touched by chemicals. You may not feel comfortable starting off on your new eco-adventure by using a big dose of weedkiller. There are certainly other ways of going about keeping an unused area of plot manageable without using chemicals, but they will be harder work. The best way is to dig out any large weeds such as brambles and then strim or mow the whole area. If you can subsequently mow the whole area regularly, all the other weeds should eventually die off or certainly be weakened and kept in check, and you will be left with an easily managed area of rough grass that looks neat and allows no danger of weeds flowering and setting seeds that will drift into your neighbour's plot.

SHARING A PLOT

You may be looking forward to creating your own little allotment kingdom and having complete control over your 250 sq m (2,700 sq ft), but if you have friends who are also interested in allotment gardening, consider the benefits of a communal approach. There are two ways of sharing your plot, and each has its benefits and drawbacks. First, you could share a full plot with a friend, half and half. This has the benefit of giving each of you a manageable area and complete autonomy over the crops, layout and approach on your own little patch.

The second way is to both work the same plot. This can be a great way to garden. Although you will need patience and diplomacy when trying to decide exactly what to grow where, you will each bring different skills to the plot, and each be able to put in different amounts of work at different times. Two people keeping an eye on weed and pest problems are equal to more than the sum of their parts, and you will be delighted to turn up and find that a weedy area that had been bothering you is suddenly and miraculously weed free. You will get the most out of sharing with someone who is at a different stage of life to you. You may be young and fit and full of energy, but perhaps you work full time and can only put in your hours at the weekends. In that case, sharing with a retired person who can pop in daily to keep on top of the day-to-day tasks such as weeding and watering, but who can't manage the more physical tasks, is perfect. Even two families are

likely to have different patterns of work and play and be able to contribute different things to a plot.

One of the greatest benefits in sharing is that you have someone to look after the plot during holiday times. These often fall over the warm summer months when vegetables (and weeds) most need your attention, and an overgrown allotment plot full of marrows instead of courgettes, and stringy old beans instead of fresh young ones, is not great to come home to. Having someone to eat the produce as it ripens – so encouraging the production of new leaves and fruits for you to eat on your return – is just as important as having someone to water and weed. You may dislike the idea of having to share your crops, but it is likely that there will always be more than enough to go around, especially if you plan ahead.

PLANNING THE LAYOUT

There are various ways of dividing up a plot. Some people go for a scorched earth policy and make the whole plot into one large bare field. This makes a plot very flexible, as you can really plant anything anywhere, but it doesn't look great. Moving around the plot after wet weather can also be tricky and you will need lots of planks of wood to walk on to avoid compressing the soil and damaging its structure. The opposite extreme is to divide the plot up into small beds, with paths running in between. The beds could

OPPOSITE If you share a plot, there's always someone to cut the grass when you are on holiday

be square ones that can be reached from all sides, or you could make a series of ten or fifteen long beds that run the width of the plot, with paths in between. Doing this would prevent you from ever having to step directly on to the soil. It makes the plot very navigable, no matter what the weather, and ensures that the soil is always in good condition. However, putting so many beds in is a lot of work, they cut down on the space you have available for planting, and they make the space fairly inflexible.

Leaving aside any extra space you may want for a cut flower garden, children's garden, seating area or wild area (these are covered in detail in chapter 10), consider dividing the majority of your plot into two unequal parts, along its width. Put over roughly a third to permanent plantings, such as soft fruit, fruit trees, asparagus beds and rhubarb plants. The rest is for annual vegetables. It is a good idea to divide this main vegetable area roughly into four. This will enable you to carry out a growing system known as rotation.

The idea of crop rotation is not to grow the same crop, or type of crop, in the same place over subsequent years. Crops that are grown in the same place year after year suffer from a build-up in the soil of their own specific pests and diseases. Such pests and diseases are often able to overwinter in the soil and get a head start in spring if their favourite food (your crop) is planted just where they emerge. To avoid this, you could just alternate crops – one year on, one year off – in the same place, but it is better to give the pests and diseases a little longer to die off or slope off elsewhere. A four-year rotation is thought to be the minimum required for healthy crops. Grouping crops also means that you can apply soil treatments specific to the requirements of each crop to a whole bed, such as well-rotted manure for legumes and lime for brassicas, rather than having to treat small individual areas. The four crop groups are: alliums (onions), brassicas (cabbages, broccoli), legumes (peas and beans), and roots and tubers. You will find more information on the practice of rotation in chapter 6, but you need to think about how you will incorporate rotation into your plot when you start planning. It is easier to adhere to a crop rotation plan if your plot is divided up into individual beds, as mentioned previously.

Consider dividing the area for annual vegetables into four long, thin beds. Some crops particularly suit this kind of layout: potatoes need to be grown in trenches and then earthed up, and it is simpler to dig one long trench than several smaller ones; beans need a support to grow up and it is easiest to create one large structure in a line than several smaller ones; and anything that needs to be covered in fleece or netting, such as the brassicas, will be easiest to grow in a long , thin bed, for the simple reason that such fabrics are usually sold in long, metre-wide strips and growing such plants in blocks can lead to frustrating time spent in complicated stitchings together. Other plants will certainly not mind being grown in a row.

Once you have made these decisions, the next thing to do is to plan it all out. There is no harm, and plenty of fun to be had, in doing this properly, using grid paper and tracing paper. First draw up a plan of your plot as accurately as you can, marking in any existing paths and structures. Then use your tracing paper to draw up several different alternatives. You might do one that keeps the shed, if there is one, where it is and makes use of existing paths, and another where you clear the whole plot and start again, putting everything exactly where you would want it in an ideal world. The final version is likely to fall somewhere between the two, but at least the process of drawing out the various possibilities will have freed you up to look at your plot afresh.

If you are allowed to have a shed, or indeed want one, site it away from any main paths, particularly any that are regularly used by cars. This will make it less attractive to vandals, who always go for the easiest, most accessible sheds first. Placing a shed, along with any other shelter and seating, further back on the plot, can make it a nice, relatively private spot from which to sit back and admire your handiwork.

A compost heap needs to be carefully sited too. It should be somewhere near the centre of the plot; otherwise you will find yourself constantly walking from one end to the other to fill it. However, it is usually best to site a compost heap away from your main seating area. If you compost correctly, a heap should not have any unpleasant smell, but sometimes they just do and it is far more pleasant not to have to sit near

it. When siting seating, bear in mind the position of your neighbours' compost, as you have even less control over the smell of their heap.

PUTTING IN PATHS

Putting in permanent paths early on is a good investment. They will help to create some order out of all the space at your disposal, and that in itself will help you to put the work you need to do into some order. Paths are good for providing a clean, mud-free way of moving around your plot, and will prevent you from always walking on the soil and so compacting it.

Before you start, think about the various options. The most common type of path is grass. You are likely to be clearing your plot from areas that have been taken over by grass, and so making a grass path may simply involve leaving a strip untouched when you are digging over the rest. Any paths already on your plot will also most likely be made of grass and so will just need a bit of tidying up and then some regular maintenance. Although grass paths are cheap and simple to create when starting out, there are some drawbacks. If you have had to clear other areas of grass, one drawback will be obvious to you: much of the grass on allotments is of the tough, weedy variety known as couch grass, which spreads by creeping into uncolonized areas, such as your newly dug-out beds. Grass paths that are simply cut from existing grassy areas will need constant maintenance and vigilance if they are not to be quickly covered in weeds. They will need regular mowing and edging, and you will need to continually pull out the little blades of grass that pop up near the edges of your beds, as well as the running roots that have taken them there. One way around this is to create paths from scratch with new turf; it will quickly begin to look like all the other grass on the site. They will still need mowing and edging but should not grow quite as vigorously and will not be such a bad source of weed infestation. All grass paths harbour slugs and snails, and that can become a real problem for your plants: slugs will hide in grass and under the edges of paths during the day, and then crawl out at night to chomp any tasty emerging young shoots, such as seedlings that you have just planted out.

You may conclude that you will make life easier for yourself in the long run if you create paths from hard landscaping materials, such as patio paving stones or gravel. Although this means more of an investment of time, energy and money when starting out, it will cut down on both maintenance and potential problems. If you are using patio pavers, you will simply need to level the path area and place them on top of the earth; there is no need to use mortar and a bed of sand on the allotment as you would were you laying a patio or path at home. If the pavers are adjacent to an area of grass that will need to be regularly mown or strimmed, dig the area out so that they sink down to the same level as the grass. This will mean that you'll be able to run a mower straight over the edges without damage.

If you choose to go for a loose path material such as gravel, park chippings, clinker or even cockle shells, it is a good idea to lay a weed-suppressing fabric underneath (this is sometimes known as landscape fabric). This should be porous, so that it lets moisture through (you don't want rainwater forming big puddles on your paths, as it would if you used thick plastic or a similar material), but it should be thick enough to exclude all light, so that weed seeds beneath it do not germinate, or cannot thrive if they do. You can spread your path materials direct on to this membrane, although you might also consider edging the path with strips of wood, in order to keep the contents neat and tidy. An added benefit of sharp materials such as shells and gravel is that they create inhospitable environments for slugs and snails, which cannot crawl over them comfortably, and so such paths are less likely to harbour anything that will crawl out and cause havoc when your back is turned.

Another option to consider right at the start is raised beds. The effectiveness of these will depend on your soil type and on what you want to grow. You create a raised bed by framing a bed with planks or strips of wood, usually held in place with wedges of wood driven into the soil, and then filling it with topsoil and manure, compost or whatever other well-rotted bulky organic matter you have available. Among the benefits is the fact that raised beds warm up

Paths create order out of chaos and make moving around the plot easy and mud free

faster in spring than the rest of the soil does, and this can mean that seeds germinate earlier and therefore you can get crops sooner than you would otherwise. They are also particularly useful if you want to control the soil type in order to grow crops that do not do well in your normal soil. My own plot is on a very heavy clay soil and it is hard to grow crops that require good drainage. A raised area filled with topsoil, with plenty of grit mixed in for extra drainage, provides the perfect environment for herbs such as thyme, oregano and even basil, which would quickly perish if planted direct into the thick clay. By filling a raised bed with an acidic, ericaceous soil you could also grow plants such as blueberries, which thrive in such conditions, in an area with a predominantly alkaline soil, in which blueberries would perish. Where raised beds become less useful is on well-drained soils, where they can have a tendency to dry out far more quickly than surrounding soil, causing problems for the plants within them and creating extra work for you.

Although it is on this sort of small scale that raised beds may be most practical for most people, it is possible to put your whole plot over to them. You would benefit from this particularly if you have a troublesome, heavy soil, or if you have mobility or back problems, as raised beds bring the area to be tended slightly closer to you. If you really struggle to bend, ask your allotment secretary about the possibility of creating more permanent, brick or wood structures to bring the soil up to waist height.

Some allotment societies are particularly open to this as a way of keeping older or less able people on their plots; there may be some raised beds set aside strictly for their use, or practical help may be available instead.

Simple wooden edges will define your beds. Although they will not have any effect on the make up of the soil within them, they are good for keeping back weeds with running root systems such as couch grass, which can gradually creep on to beds. They are another tool for making the plot easier to manage.

ESSENTIAL TOOLS

Before you get started, set yourself up with some tools. You will need a spade, fork, rake, hoe, hand fork and trowel. These are the basics, and they will pretty well cover you for most jobs. Some extras to consider include a cultivator – a three-pronged instrument that you drag through the soil and can use for a great number of jobs, including grubbing up weeds and creating a fine tilth in which to direct sow seeds. If you are of small build, or find digging hard going, look out for a border spade. This is much more petite than a normal spade and, although the going can be a little slower as each spadeful of earth is much smaller, it can make much lighter work of a hefty digging job. You will need, too, a pair of shears to keep your grass paths and edges neat, and a watering can; see also page 143.

Raised beds create well-drained vegetable beds that look good and are easy to work and weed

3

DECIDING WHAT TO GROW

You may already have a list, either in your head or on paper, of the crops you want to grow on your plot. When following the half-hour system, in which you are trying to grow your crops with the minimum input of time, it is a good idea to learn the simplest ways of growing each crop before you begin. These ways will not always be the cheapest, but they will save you time and effort. This is also the stage at which to refine your list and to look at the realities of growing each crop, and whether crops are good or bad value in terms of the space and attention they will demand.

When you have first cleared your plot, the space available to you will seem endless. This will be especially true if you are used to the confines of a small town garden or courtyard. Even a half or a quarter allotment will stretch away from you, making you feel that you will never fill it up. You will be surprised at how wrong this impression is. Plants take up space. You are likely to make plans for growing a huge variety of crops, and then find, come May, that you have filled up all the space you have available and have to give away all your beautiful tomato plants to neighbours. If you have a reduced plot, say a half or a quarter of a traditional plot, space will be at a particular premium and in order to be able to manage it more easily you will need to make every plant work hard.

A plant can be bad value, in the context of the half-hour plot, for a number of reasons. Perhaps it takes up a lot of space over a long amount of time before cropping, or does not produce high

yields. It may be prey to particularly virulent pests and diseases and so demand a lot of effort to make it produce good-quality crops; or it may be cheap and easily accessible from shops, and so not worth the effort of growing. Few crops will be all these things, and you will have to weigh up these factors with your love for the final product. An interesting example is purple-sprouting broccoli. This has major drawbacks. The main problem is that the plant is big and needs to be in the ground for a long period of time. Plants planted out in late spring need almost 1 sq m (10 sq ft) each, and they will not crop until the following late winter or early spring, and then only for a few weeks. On the other hand, the crop is extremely tasty, expensive to buy and difficult to find in the shops. To decide whether to grow it, you must weigh up the pros and cons, depending on the space you have available. Some other winter brassicas have the same problems, most notably white sprouting broccoli and cauliflower; on the other hand, cabbages are fairly quick to mature and easy to grow, and Brussels sprouts, although large plants, can be picked over a long period of time. Perhaps the best-value crop of this group is curly kale, an excellent substitute for purple-sprouting broccoli if you have to make the choice; it is tasty, hard to get hold of and fairly expensive in the shops, yet it matures quickly and crops over a long period of time.

In several cases it is worth considering alternatives. Peas are tricky to grow, partly

Lettuces are the ultimate good-value crop: they take up little space, are fast growing and taste best when they are really fresh

because they are martyrs to pests such as pea moth and pea and bean weevil. But the main factor counting against growing them is that they are cheap to buy. Of course, popping a freshly picked raw pea into your mouth is an entirely different experience from eating frozen peas, but once peas are cooked and combined with other foods in a dish, can you really tell the difference? And is that difference important enough for it to be worth going to all the effort involved in growing these tricky and demanding plants? On the other hand, mangetout is a gourmet ingredient that can be hard to find in the shops and always extremely expensive when you do. The plants are much smaller and highly productive and do not involve the same level of pest and disease heartache that you suffer when growing peas. Peas, therefore, are low value and mangetout high value.

Onions are low value. Although they are pretty easy to grow and do not take up too much space, they are so cheap to buy that growing them is a false economy. They are certainly not as suitable for a time- and space-limited gardener as spring onions and shallots. While just as easy to grow and taking up almost identical amounts of space, both of these are far more interesting crops and have more unusual flavours and applications, as well as being expensive and less easy to find in the shops.

One crop over which there can be little argument is maincrop potatoes. These are so cheap to buy in the shops that it seems pointless to grow them on an allotment. They take up loads of space in the ground where you could be growing some really interesting crops such as aubergines or melons. They are also a pain after harvest, as they need to be stored and so take up indoor space. This is all very well if you have a garage or garden shed at your disposal, but if you live in a small flat they will end up wedged down the side of the washing machine or balanced on top of the wardrobe. Unless you are planning to use them as a method of weed clearance (see page 76), go out and buy them instead.

So those are some really bad-value plants. What are the good ones? For a plant to be good value, you are looking for something that germinates easily, matures quickly and with few problems from pests and diseases, and takes up little space. Most importantly, a good-value plant is one that really needs to be eaten fresh to be best appreciated. Mixed salad leaves and lettuce must be the ultimate good-value crop. They are at their crisp and juicy best when freshly harvested, rather than bought in sweaty supermarket packets; they germinate and mature incredibly quickly, and take up little space; and they taste great. They can also be squeezed, both physically and temporally, between other crops, either in small rows between slow-growing crops or filling a space where something else is due to be planted later.

Dwarf French beans are high scorers too, because they are expensive to buy, each plant is compact and hugely productive, and once they are in the ground they involve almost no care.

New potatoes have one distinct edge over their maincrop relatives: they are high value mainly because they really must be eaten fresh out of the ground. This is the crop that deteriorates the most once harvested and, no matter how hard they try, supermarkets and greengrocers will never be able to match the freshness and taste that you get when you pull a handful of new potatoes out of the ground, take them home and boil them that evening.

While it might be helpful to bear in mind which plants are really good value, don't let it be the only criterion you employ. The most important thing is to choose and grow plants that you love to eat. If you hate mangetout and love purple-sprouting broccoli, then grow purple-sprouting broccoli you must. This should be the golden rule: grow vegetables that you love to eat. A surprising proportion of allotmenteers grow crops because they are given seed, or they think they are proper 'allotment plants', and then end up giving them all away to their neighbours.

SEED OR PLANT?

For some, vegetable growing is irrevocably tied to the process of sowing and germinating your own seedlings. There is something life-affirming about nurturing a plant from seed; the first sign of a shoot pushing its way through the earth is a truly heart-warming moment.

However, one of the problems with growing vegetables from seed is that you always end up with too many. Seed packets usually contain

enough seeds for several gardeners, but seeds will not keep indefinitely and become less reliable at germinating if kept over several years. If you try to grow each and every seed in each packet you buy, you will end up with hundreds of plants. If you don't, there will be a lot of waste.

Indoor seed sowing is an incredible amount of fuss. Most new allotmenteers, trying to fit a little vegetable growing around a busy lifestyle and with little space at their disposal, will not have invested in a greenhouse. If this is the case for you, you will end up with every windowsill and table in your house groaning with seedlings. Equally, you can put in many hours of effort and still end up with an inferior plant or none at all. There is the initial sowing, quickly followed by pricking out. If you don't do this soon enough, you will end up with leggy seedlings with their roots matted together. Pricking out is a massive job involving hours of your time, huge numbers of pots and volumes of compost, as well as requiring the expertise to do it well without snapping off all the precious roots. Without a greenhouse, you will spend most of mid- and late spring avidly watching the weather forecast and hoicking your more tender seedlings such as tomatoes and pumpkins in and out, while running the risk that one day you will forget and lose the lot.

Some hardier crops can be sown in a nursery bed on the allotment and then put into place at a later date. Although this is not quite as tricky as windowsill propagation, it has its drawbacks. You will still end up with many more plants than you

need. Plants grown in a nursery bed always have their roots disturbed or even broken when they are moved to their permanent positions, and this can seriously set them back. A nursery bed is also a feature for those with the luxury of space, and if you are to use every inch as efficiently as possible, it has no place on your plot.

The answer is wonderfully straightforward: get someone else to grow your seedlings for you. Seed companies have only relatively recently caught on to the potential of making vegetable plug plants available to amateur gardeners, but this is a development we should embrace wholeheartedly. The companies that do this are experts. They grow plants perfectly and supply them in fabulous condition. They take on all the fiddly bits such as sowing and pricking out. They take on the risk of frost and make sure that plants are grown in glasshouses when they need to be, and that they get plenty of light, water and food. If they grow plants that look a bit rough, you don't buy them, whereas if you grow such plants yourself you are stuck with them. Some companies will even supply plants at the moment at which they should be planted out. This means that you only have to think about what you want to grow at the beginning of the year when you order them, and that you don't have to spend time plotting and planning and working out how to get things into the ground at the right time. The plants just turn up on your doorstep at the correct moment and you nip up to the allotment and pop them into the ground.

In simple monetary terms, plug plants are more expensive than plants grown from seed. But this is one point where the needs of the half-hour gardener are at odds with traditional allotment values. As I said earlier, there is no shame in spending a little money on your allotment. You might well spend far more on any other hobby you might take up, and there are occasions, such as this, when spending a little frees up so much time and spares you so much bother that it is worth it.

You may reach a stage, a few years down the line, when you itch to try lots of heritage or unusual cultivars, and the companies that supply plug plants no longer offer enough variety for you. This is one of the drawbacks of relying on others to start your plants off for you: you cannot choose exactly which cultivar to grow, as you would if you bought seeds from a seed catalogue and grew them yourself. When you reach that point, you will have to decide whether you are prepared to put in the extra time and effort involved in growing from seed in order to expand you horizons in this way. Until then, plug plants will help you though the first few years, and give you the confidence to experiment. (Sowing seeds in seed trays and then planting out is discussed on page 149.)

Plug plants are not always the answer, but there are a few situations in which they definitely come out on top. Use them whenever

OPPOSITE Buying plug plants can free up a huge amount of time and ensure that you start off with well-grown seedlings

you need only a few plants in order to get a good crop. Examples might include courgettes, a few plants of which produce enough fruits to feed a whole street, let alone your family and friends. Use plug plants wherever you would otherwise need heat or shelter to produce frost-tender seedlings such as tomatoes through the early part of the year. And choose them above seed sowing whenever plants need to be well spaced apart, as with brassicas.

Although onion and shallot sets are a slightly different matter, it is always worth choosing these over seed too if you are trying to grow vegetables in a limited amount of time and space. You will have less choice of cultivar, but set-grown onions need be in the ground for a far shorter period of time than seed-grown ones, and planting sets is much less fuss than sowing and planting out seed.

When you are starting off, you should be able to buy all the plug plants you need from a garden centre, where they should be in good condition and supplied at the right time for planting out. However, you will never know whether the garden centre will have the plant that you want and you may find that they have sold out. The number of cultivars on offer will also be limited. Specialist vegetable plug plant suppliers will be able to offer a far greater range of cultivars and ordering from them is a way of guaranteeing that you get exactly the plants you want. These companies often supply by mail order, and the smaller outfits are often better tuned to the needs of the allotmenteer. For a list of mail order suppliers, see page 156.

SEED SOWING

There is still a place for seed sowing on a half-hour allotment, and that is when they can be sown direct into the ground. As a general rule, the half-hour allotmenteer should only buy seed that can be direct sown. Sowing in this way is far removed from the palaver and inconvenience of sowing in pots or trays indoors (see page 148) or even sowing into a nursery bed. It is used for plants that grow well from seed that is just shoved into the ground at the right time, such as French and broad beans. It is also useful for crops that are grown close together – a good guide is to direct sow those that grow closer than 15cm (6in) to each other. These include carrots, spring onions, beetroot, parsnip and mixed leaf lettuces. Although plug plants are always more expensive, in these cases, buying the number of plants that you would need would

Direct sowing in a straight line makes it easier to distinguish germinating weeds from vegetable seedlings

be ridiculously so, and the trouble involved in planting each out individually would far outweigh that of sowing seed. All of these are best sown in drills, left to germinate and then thinned to the correct spacing. This is far better for the plants than being sown in nursery beds and then yanked up and placed in their final positions. It means that those that you leave behind will have an intact and undisturbed root system.

There are some disadvantages to direct sowing. One is the need to thin out your seedlings once they have germinated. No matter how hard you try to sow your seeds thinly, there will always be some need for thinning. If you tried to place seeds of, say, beetroot exactly 10cm (4in) apart, not only could you not manage do so evenly but some would be bound not to germinate, and you would be left with gaps. In some cases, as with close-sown carrots, the thinnings themselves are edible; raw carrot thinnings make a lovely, sweet, crunchy addition to salads.

Although thinning out can seem like extra work, it gives you the chance to get down on the ground near your seedlings, and provides a good opportunity to weed them thoroughly. Weeding can be a little tricky with direct-sown seeds, as weed seedlings and vegetable seedlings are likely to germinate at the same time and look very similar, at least at first. One of the best ways around this is to sow in lines, rather than to scatter the seed across a larger area. A definite line of seedlings will germinate and you will know that they are probably your vegetables, not weeds, and you can then weed all around them. As you become more experienced, you will be able to differentiate between weed seedlings and your vegetable seedlings, but when you are first starting out, leave everything in the line until the seedlings start to look different from each other.

Another problem with seed sowing is the constant, preying presence of dreaded slugs and snails. These exist on every allotment in huge numbers and love eating tender, juicy seedlings above all else. Unhindered, they can be devastating, wiping out rows of seedlings in a single night. You will need to protect any directly sown seedlings from them. For information on dealing with pests, see chapter 8.

PERENNIAL PLANTS

When it comes to evaluating perennial vegetable and fruit plants, things get a little complicated. You might think that they are low-value plants because they take up so much space all year round and have relatively short cropping seasons. But although they are great space hoggers, their permanence is part of their attractiveness for the gardener with limited time. Once perennial plants are in and established, they need only the minimum amount of care to keep on producing crop after crop. You need to maintain them, true, but you will never need to think about sowing them or buying in plants again, until the time comes to replace them, and that can be very many years

later. On a small plot you may feel you don't have space for perennial plants, but if you do decide to give an area of your plot to them, it will be almost self-maintaining.

Another reason for growing perennial crops is that almost all of them produce really luxurious crops. An allotment without raspberries would be a sad place. Although they are big plants, they are incredibly easy to grow and utterly delicious. The same goes for all the other soft fruit: loganberries, strawberries, gooseberries, rhubarb, redcurrants and blackcurrants all make delicious, vitamin-packed additions to a family's menu and all are ridiculously easy to care for. Asparagus takes up lots of space, but it is so delicious and so expensive to buy in that it would seem a real shame to miss it out.

If space is really limited, there are ways that you can squeeze these crops in. There are some, such as rhubarb and asparagus, that cannot be trained or encouraged to grow in any way other than the obvious. But both soft and tree fruit can be trained so that they take up only a little space on the ground.

Not all allotment societies allow fruit trees, mainly because of concerns that they will grow too large and shade neighbouring plots, so you need to check the rules before you start buying and planting. Fruit trees can grow incredibly large, and they can be a problem if gardeners don't know what they are looking for when they buy and then let them grow freely. However, they are also easily controlled, and in fact produce more fruit when they are forced to stay compact.

With fruit trees for confined areas, the most important factor is the rootstock. All fruit trees that you will find in garden centres or from specialist suppliers are grafted on to a rootstock, rather than on their own roots. Rootstocks control the vigour of the plant, so whereas an apple cultivar grown on an MM111 rootstock might grow up to 10m (30ft) in height, the same grafted on to an M27 rootstock might reach only 2m (6ft). The largest rootstock you should go for when choosing apples is an M9, which will grow up to only 3m (10ft) even if left to grow freely. With pears, look for Quince C rootstock, and with plums and gages, go for Pixy or St Julien A.

In addition to choosing the correct rootstock, you can keep fruit trees small through training. You might think that this would severely reduce the amount of fruit that they produce, but in fact, the bends and corners that are required to

ABOVE Apple trees need not take up lots of room. When space is really tight you can train them along fences

OPPOSITE Once established, rhubarb almost takes care of itself, and it produces large amounts of tasty crops each year

make the plant grow in a particular shape force the sap to move more slowly through the plant, and this leads to more tough, fruiting growth being formed, at the expense of the lush, sappy green growth that the tree would put on if allowed to grow freely. Top-fruit trees, such as apples, cherries, peaches, pears and plums, can be trained as espaliers, cordons or fans, all of which keep the growth on a strictly vertical plane. This means that they hardly take up any precious allotment space, and can even be grown along the boundaries. A really neat way to grow apples is as stepovers. These comprise a single horizontal branch, growing on a leg; they are therefore very low growing and can be stepped over. They make wonderful edging plants for beds and boundaries. You can either buy trees as young plants and train them yourself, using a system of wires, or you can buy plants that are several years old and have already been trained into various shapes. This is an expensive way of going about it, but very convenient, and will give you an instant effect. As well as being productive, trained fruit trees look beautiful and can be a real feature on your plot.

Soft fruit, such as blackcurrants and raspberries, can also be trained to make it fit into your limited space more snugly. You should

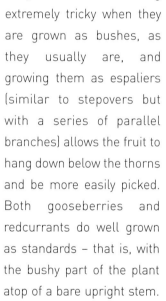

certainly grow plants such as loganberries, blackberries and raspberries along a fence or a system of wires, so that they take up only a limited amount of space on a very strict plane. It is less commonly done, but there is no reason at all why gooseberries should not be grown as cordons, espaliers or fans. In fact, the sharp thorns of the gooseberry often make harvesting extremely tricky when they are grown as bushes, as they usually are, and growing them as espaliers (similar to stepovers but with a series of parallel branches) allows the fruit to hang down below the thorns and be more easily picked. Both gooseberries and redcurrants do well grown as standards – that is, with the bushy part of the plant atop of a bare upright stem. Again, the fruit can hang down and be more easily picked, and growing them this way also allows plenty of air circulation around the base of the plant, and that is good for helping to keep down fungal diseases. It is a great example of the way you can manipulate plants in order to fit more into your plot, while increasing productivity and plant health at the same time.

ABOVE Raspberries may be fairly large plants but they are worth growing as their fruits are at their most juicy and delicious when eaten freshly picked

RIGHT Plums look good, crop well and take up little space when they are trained into fans, cordons and espaliers

4

GROWING THE RIGHT AMOUNT OF THE BEST VARIETIES

One of the main reasons most people bother with this whole allotment business, rather than simply buying fruit and veg from a supermarket, is that they think that home-grown food tastes better than commercially grown food. But the unfortunate truth is that tastier food does not come automatically with owning an allotment or vegetable patch. It is still possible to produce bland crops, or get bored because you have grown too much of one crop and have had to eat them night after night for two months.

GROWING THE RIGHT CULTIVARS

If you know why produce sold by supermarkets is so bland, you can easily avoid producing bland food yourself. Firstly, supermarkets cannot easily get produce on the shelves in less than two days, and it is therefore picked before it is quite ripe, which can affect flavour and freshness. Secondly, commercial growers often put lots of resources into protecting their plants and giving them lots of water, particularly in the case of tomatoes, peppers, cucumbers and aubergines. This is called growing them 'soft' and takes such a high level of resources that it would be impossible for most amateur vegetable growers to grow this way. It produces large and perfect-looking crops, but waters down the flavour if the produce is not allowed to ripen properly. Although supermarkets are attempting to

adapt to their customers' demands for better flavour, the majority of commercial growers grow the cultivars that are most amenable to this sort of treatment, and the ones that are most likely to look good and produce the highest yields, even if they are not necessarily the best tasting.

High yield should not be a defining issue on the half-hour plot, where the idea is not to be self-sufficient but to supplement your diet with tasty, fresh and nutritious food, and to amaze your dinner-party guests with the intensity of its flavours. Look for specialist seed merchants who are likely to advise you on the tastiest crops that are well suited to allotment growing. Your carrots may not be the vibrant orange of the supermarket carrots, but they will probably taste far sweeter. Your strawberry plants may produce only a few handfuls of fruits each compared with the pounds of fruit from a commercial cultivar, but those few that you get are far more likely to taste 'as strawberries used to taste'.

Talk to your allotment neighbours about which cultivars they grow. They may not have looked into alternatives to commercial cultivars, but the chances are that they have come across a few unusual favourites, particularly if they have been at it for a few years. They will also be able to tell you what crops grow particularly well on your site, and equally what not to bother with. Learn from their successes and failures, rather than forcing yourself to learn from your own.

FEAST AND FAMINE

Most allotment holders will be familiar with the experience of suddenly having to deal with a glut of certain vegetables. This is generally seen as an acceptable and slightly comical aspect of allotment growing, but in fact with the right approach it can be avoided. The real problem with a glut is that it means that you will probably not eat your vegetables when they are at their best. If you grow a 10m (30ft) row of French beans, for instance, they will all reach perfect harvesting stage – when they are just a few inches long and still tender and tasty – at the same time. As soon as they are ready, you will harvest the first few plants, which will give you enough beans for two or three meals, which is probably all you want for that week. The next few plants will probably still be all right to harvest the following week, but all this time the beans at the end of the row will be getting tougher and stringier. By the time you reach them, you will probably be so fed up of beans that you throw them all on the compost heap.

The typical allotment is the equivalent of an American-style all-you-can-eat restaurant that leaves you stuffed and heavy and swearing that you will never eat again. What we want to aim for is the fine French restaurant experience, where the portions are small but utterly delicious, and where you are left slightly wanting at the end of the meal. Remember: you do not have the time to aim for self-sufficiency,

but you can use your allotment to inject taste and interest into your diet.

The technique for growing just enough crops to keep you almost satisfied is simple. You sow or plant smaller amounts, and in some cases you sow these small amounts successionally, over a period of time, so that separate sowings of the same crop come to the perfect point of ripeness every few weeks, rather than a huge amount being ready at once. Once crops are ready, you pick little and often.

WHAT TO GROW, HOW MUCH TO GROW AND HOW TO GROW IT

Although that sounds straightforward, it is little help if you have never grown the crop before and have no idea how much is too much. The table on pages 50–73 is designed to help you decide how much you need to sow, or how many plants you need to plant, in order to feed a typical family of four. Amend these figures according to the amount of people you need to feed and, of course, to suit your own tastes. If you really love a particular crop, and are likely to eat it every day when it is in season, you will need to grow more. There are tips on how best to get a good succession of young, tender vegetables from each crop. In addition, the table tells you whether the crop is easiest grown from plants purchased at the garden centre or through specialist growers, or if it is simpler to sow it direct.

Not every vegetable is included in this table. It covers only those crops that Will Sibley and I consider good-value crops for the half-hour plot. The criteria for this vary from crop to crop, but each has at least one of the following attributes:

- it is a gourmet vegetable that is particularly tasty
- it is hard to track down in the shops or expensive to buy
- it takes up little room on the plot, or does not need to be in the ground over a long period of time
- it is particularly easy to grow.

If you really must grow maincrop potatoes and ordinary onions, I'm afraid you will have to find information about them elsewhere. The tips outlined for growing each crop are not necessarily the definitive techniques – for many crops there may well be many other methods you could use – but they are the techniques that we consider the most productive for gardeners with small plots and limited time to spend on them.

It is better to grow a few plants of lots of different crops than to eat the same thing each day, all through the season

← APPLES	ASPARAGUS
Plant only those grafted on to dwarf rootstocks (M9 or M27) and buy these trained as cordons or stepovers so that they stay compact and do not take up too much space.	Takes up lots of space on an allotment, but too tasty to miss out on. Perennial, so pretty straightforward to maintain once established after two or three years.
Plant	Crowns
Three stepovers or cordons	Ten crowns
Choose a selection of disease-resistant cultivars for a succession of ripening times and to ensure cross-pollination	Cut at least every other day from when spears start to emerge
Plant when trees are dormant in a sunny, sheltered site. Prune in winter, shortening side growths from the main stems to create many fruiting spurs	Plant in early spring into very free-draining soil. Plants must be left to grow for two or three years before you start to cut them. From mid-spring for a duration of six to eight weeks, harvest spears that are sticking out of the ground by 12–18cm (5–7in), cutting 2.5cm (1in) below soil level to get blanched stems. Enjoys seaweed fertilizer
'Pinova' (early September ripening), 'Park Farm Pippin' (end September), 'Red Falstaff' (end October)	Choose all-male cultivars that will not go to seed, such as 'Backlim', 'Gijnlim', 'Jersey Knight'

AUBERGINE	BEANS, BROAD	BEANS, DWARF FRENCH	GOOD-VALUE ALLOTMENT CROPS
Very tasty, but will grow only in the sunniest, most sheltered site outdoors. Elsewhere, grow under the protection of a cloche, cold frame, greenhouse or polytunnel. There are several unusual cultivars that you cannot find in the shops.	Delicious when small and a very good early crop.	Dwarf cultivars are incredibly easy to grow, requiring no support and almost no attention but producing lots of beans over a long period.	
Plants	Seed	Seed	**PLANT OR SEED?**
Three plants of different cultivars to give a variety of shapes and harvest times	Two 3m (10ft) rows	Two 3m (10ft) rows	**HOW MUCH?**
Regular picking before the fruits are too large encourages more fruits to appear	Best eaten when young and tender, so sow at intervals and pick when small. Autumn sowing produces tougher plants that are less susceptible to attack by blackfly, but the seed may rot over winter in heavy soils	Sow at intervals during growing season to produce beans from June to end September. Pick every third day to keep pods young and tender	**TIPS**
Plants should arrive around May, and they should be planted out then but kept under cloches until the end of June. Grow in your sunniest and warmest spot. Put cloches back on as weather cools to ripen the last few	Direct sow seed in autumn or spring 22cm (9in) apart. Pinch out the tips of blackfly-infested plants when the flowers have set, as they attack and breed on the softer parts	Direct sow in an area high in moisture-retentive organic matter, as plants respond well to water. Make the first (April) sowing under cloches as seedlings are tender to frost; remove cloches when danger of frost has passed. The last sowing can be as late as mid-August. Water regularly	**GENERAL INFORMATION**
'Purple Prince', 'Slicerite', 'Mohican' (small white fruits), 'Red Egg' (colourful fruits)	'Super Aquadulce' (good for overwintering for earliest crops), 'Imperial Green Longpod' (particularly tasty)	Choose dwarf rather than climbing cultivars, as they are much easier to look after. 'Delinell' (large crops), 'Triomph de Farcy Stringless' (old gourmet type with great flavour)	**RECOMMENDED CULTIVARS**

← BEANS, RUNNER	BEETROOT →
A little fussy, as they need support, but will produce tasty beans well into autumn.	Very easy to grow, although some people may not want them as they take quite a lot of preparation to get them to the table.
Plant and seed	Seed
One 4m (12ft) row	Two 3m (10ft) rows, sown at intervals
Pick every three days from July until late September	Easy to grow but can have a tendency to bolt in dry weather, so keep well watered. When harvesting, twist rather than cut the leaves off to minimize bleeding
Construct a solid support. Add plenty of organic matter to soil to retain moisture. Buy your first lot as plants and plant out 30cm (12in) apart, in May. At the same time sow two seeds between each plant (one may not germinate or may be eaten). This allows a succession of plants without the need to construct a new support for the second sowing. Water well throughout season	Direct sow at intervals, with first row in late February. Thin to 10cm (4in) apart when seedlings large enough. Repeat with second sowing in June. Start picking when golf-ball sized from May through the winter
'Red Rum' (particularly tasty), 'White Lady' (lovely tender pods), 'Scarlet Emperor' (old favourite)	'Boltardy' (resistant to bolting), 'Detroit Globe' (best flavoured, sweet, almost black flesh)

BROCCOLI AND CALABRESE	BRUSSELS SPROUTS	GOOD-VALUE ALLOTMENT CROPS
Delicious, mature very quickly and have antioxidant properties.	Controversial: some people hate them but to others they are delicious. Can be picked over a long period of time.	
Plants	Plants	**PLANT OR SEED?**
Twenty per planting, three plantings	Twelve plants	**HOW MUCH?**
Lots of plants are necessary as each produces a fairly small head	Brussels sprouts are supposed to get sweeter and have the best taste after they have been subjected to the first frost. Pick as you need them over long period of time	**TIPS**
Plant 30–60cm (12–24in) apart in rows. First planting in April, second in June and third in August. Final planting will overwinter. Protect from birds, particularly in spring. Likes a warm spot	Plant out in May. Normally plants are placed at 1m (3ft) intervals, but closer spacing at 38cm (15in) allows them to support each other and prevents wind rock. For best winter crops, keep well watered throughout summer	**GENERAL INFORMATION**
Calabrese: 'Belstar' (good flavour), 'Trixie' (said to be high in antioxidants), 'Hydra' (produces sideshoots once main head is cut) Sprouting broccoli: 'Early Purple Sprouting Improved', 'Late Purple Sprouting', 'White Eye' (white, early sprouting)	'Noisette' (old, nutty-flavoured cultivar), 'Cromwell' (short growing, low wind resistance), 'Red Delicious' (unusual red-coloured sprouts)	**RECOMMENDED CULTIVARS**

← CABBAGE, SPRING

Very tasty and welcome in spring.

Plants

Twelve plants

Pick and eat as required

Planted in autumn, 12in (30cm) apart, plants should be ready to harvest from following March to the end of May

'Pixie' (tasty, pointed type), 'Hispi' (good taste, pointed type)

CABBAGE, WINTER	CARROTS →		GOOD-VALUE ALLOTMENT CROPS
Easy to grow and tasty.	Easy-to-produce crop for the whole year. Sweet and tasty.		
Plants	Seed		PLANT OR SEED?
Ten plants	3m (10ft) rows sown every three weeks during growing season		HOW MUCH?
Pick as required through winter	When pencil thick, thin out every other one to eat raw in salads. Eat the rest as required. August sowings can be eaten throughout winter – you may want to sow a couple of rows for this purpose		TIPS
Plant out in June into well-manured ground. Can be particularly susceptible to cabbage white butterflies and pigeons. Harvest from end October throughout winter	Direct sow seed thinly in succession with first sowing in February and repeat at three-weekly intervals until August. Thin plants to 2.5cm (1in) apart and discard thinnings. Give lots of water throughout summer. Harvest small carrots by wiggling the tops until the roots loosen: lifting with a fork will disturb too many plants. If carrots are hard to pull, water ten minutes before harvesting. Protect from carrot fly		GENERAL INFORMATION
Savoy varieties are the tastiest: 'January King' (best-flavoured Savoy and very hardy, but not as crinkly leaved as some), 'Tundra' (the hardiest cabbage and good for cold areas)	'Primo' (earliest for first sowing of year), 'Early Nantes' (all year round), 'Nanco' (for August sowings to stand into winter), 'Paris Market' (globe type, good on clay soils), 'Sytan' (carrot fly resistance)		RECOMMENDED CULTIVARS

CAULIFLOWER	CELERIAC
A good tasty crop, but avoid growing too many.	Harder to find in the shops and far more expensive than celery, but easier to grow and with a similar taste. Delicious mashed together with potato.
Plants	Plants
Six plants	Eight plants
Plants produce large heads, so you can quickly get tired of them if you go for too many plants	Plants grow huge – up to 1kg (2lb) each – so don't grow too many
Plant out in June to harvest from November/December onwards. Harvest throughout winter as required	Plant out in June and harvest from late October to the end of March as required. Likes lots of water through the growing season and hates getting dried out
'Castlegrant'	'Monarch'

← CHARD	CHICORY	GOOD-VALUE ALLOTMENT CROPS
Highly productive, has a delicate flavour and is a colourful addition to the kitchen. Use leaf or stalk steamed or stir-fried, or use the young leaves in salads.	Tasty winter salad crop.	
Seed	Seed	**PLANT OR SEED?**
Two 3m (10ft) rows	One 3m (10ft) row	**HOW MUCH?**
Tolerant of most conditions and treatment. Will regrow several times after cutting	For the best-quality leaves, grow under cloches in winter	**TIPS**
Direct sow first row in March and second in August for continuity of leaves. Thin seedlings to 15cm (6in) apart and start cutting, with scissors, as soon as large enough	Sow direct into the row in May and thin out seedlings to 15cm (6in) apart. Harvest throughout winter as required	**GENERAL INFORMATION**
'Bright Lights' (colourful stems), 'White Silver' (pure white stems and dark green leaves)	'Jupiter' (red), 'Palla Rossa' (traditional red), 'Witloof' (good for forcing)	**RECOMMENDED CULTIVARS**

← COURGETTES	GARLIC
Tasty, tender, essential summer crop. Delicious griddled on the barbecue or even eaten raw if picked young enough.	Essential part of much modern cooking and easy to grow. Requires drying and storing but does not take up much space.
Plants	Bulbs
Four plants	Three bulbs (up to thirty cloves)
Courgettes are the classic glut plant and each plant will make huge numbers of fruits. For the tastiest crops pick every day when the fruits are just a few inches long, or else they will soon turn into marrows	Harvest all when mature and dry to use through winter
Buy two plants and plant them in mid-May. Two weeks later buy two more plants and plant them out. This way not all your plants will ripen at the same time. Give plants lots of space – they will need at least 1 sq m (10 sq ft) each. Take care to plant out after frosts have passed, as they are very tender. Give lots of water throughout the summer.	Plant in autumn, at 18cm (7in) spacings. Requires lots of sun and good drainage. Bulbs swell up and split into cloves when they first start growing in spring, and copious watering at this time will encourage the best-quality crops. Harvest midsummer
'Kojak' (good flavour, green), 'Gold Rush' (good flavour, yellow fruits, highly productive), 'De Nice a Fruit Rond' (round, pale green fruits), 'Custard White' (white, scalloped edge)	'Thermidrome', 'Roja' (the gourmet cultivar but hard to track down), 'Solent Wight' (large bulbs, good flavour)

KALE, CURLY	LEEKS →		GOOD-VALUE ALLOTMENT CROPS
Delicious gourmet vegetable for winter steaming. Easy to grow and each plant will crop several times.	Cheap to buy but worth growing for difference in taste between home-grown crops and commercially grown crops, which are also subject to high levels of chemical sprays.		
Plants	Seed or plug plants		PLANT OR SEED?
Fifteen plants	Six 2m (6ft) rows		HOW MUCH?
When harvesting, cut the centres of the plants out to eat them as required. They will grow again	When weeding, draw a hoe between the rows to earth up young plants slightly. Begin to harvest as soon as large enough		TIPS
Plant out in June about 25cm (10in) apart, in well-drained soil. Protect from whitefly. Will put up with extremely low temperatures over winter. Harvest from September through winter	Direct sow seed at 8cm (3in) intervals in rows 30cm (12in) apart in May. This close spacing makes them tall and slim and encourages self-blanching (the stems stay white and tender rather than turning green). Harvest during winter and into spring from one end of row to the other; do not thin out or blanching effect will be lost. During mid-spring, plug plants can be dropped into small holes made with the handle of your hoe, and watered.		GENERAL INFORMATION
'Red Bor' (dark red leaves and good flavour), 'Winterbor' (green)	'Apollo' (vigorous, slim-growing leek), 'Musselburgh' (strong flavour), 'Bulgarian Giant' (particularly good for close spacing)		RECOMMENDED CULTIVARS

LETTUCE →

Easy to grow and at its best when freshly harvested. Good cut-and-come-again crop.

Seed

One 2m (6ft) row sown every four weeks

Buy a packet of mixed leaves or several packets of different types and mix them together. Use scissors to cut as much as you need each day, cutting the entire plant at around 5cm (2in) from ground. Do not store but eat immediately. Plants will re-sprout and can be cut again several times. Always cut the largest plants first

Direct sow every two weeks from March to September. Prefers a cooler spot with some shade. Keep well watered but wet the soil rather than the leaves or else the leaves will rot. Harvest as necessary

Combine with as many different types of salad leaves as you can find: cos, little gem, oak leaf, frilly and red lettuces, rocket and mustards

LOGANBERRIES AND OTHER HYBRID BERRIES	MANGETOUT AND SUGAR SNAP PEAS	GOOD-VALUE ALLOTMENT CROPS
Big cropping plants, with much higher yields than blackberries.	More expensive vegetable to buy than normal garden peas but easier to grow.	
Plant	Seed	**PLANT OR SEED?**
One plant	One 3m (10ft) double row	**HOW MUCH?**
For best-sized fruits, water as the fruit is swelling	Start picking as soon as pods are 3.5cm (1 1/2in) long	**TIPS**
Plant in late autumn in the middle of a sturdy, long-term support (two strong stakes with wires strung between). In autumn, cut the fruited stems down to the ground after harvest, and tie in two new shoots horizontally, which will bear next year's fruit	In November and again in March, direct sow into rich, well-manured ground with seeds at 15cm (6in) spacings, then another row of seeds in between but offset by the same spacing. This allows you to push twiggy supports in between for the plants to climb up. Keep soil moist by watering regularly during dry spells	**GENERAL INFORMATION**
'LY59' (loganberry), tayberry, boysenberry	'Oregon Sugar Pod' (sweet and crunchy mangetout type), 'Sugar Crystal' (snap type)	**RECOMMENDED CULTIVARS**

MELONS →

Delicious, although a greenhouse or polytunnel is essential in cool summers.

Plants or pre-chitted seed (seed is particularly hard to germinate)

Six plants

Not possible to grow a succession as we only have enough warmth long enough to grow one crop.

Plant in early summer. Need lots of water to ripen well. Pick as skins start splitting and eat immediately

'Sweetheart', 'Castella'

ORIENTAL LEAVES	PEARS	GOOD-VALUE ALLOTMENT CROPS
Unusual and varied crop that is hard to find and expensive to buy in shops. Particularly useful for stir-fries.	Grown on dwarfing rootstocks, pears can be kept relatively compact. Only grow those trained as cordons or stepovers, or else they will take up too much space.	
Seed	Plants	**PLANT OR SEED?**
Two 4m (12ft) rows	Three plants	**HOW MUCH?**
Good cut-and-come-again crop. Cut with scissors as required when plants are young and tender. Not good for summer sowings as they can bolt. Can be grown out of doors through winter or under cloches, and can be cut during this time until leaves get too stalky	Watering well for the six weeks after flowering will give big, juicy pears. Grow a variety of cultivars to ensure good pollination and a succession of ripening times	**TIPS**
Direct sow in August. It will overwinter well	Plant when dormant in a warm, sheltered site that is not in a frost pocket. Pears love water, so give as much as possible. Prune in winter to thin out damaged, diseased or overcrowded growth. Pick while still firm when they begin to change colour and ripen indoors for one to three weeks	**GENERAL INFORMATION**
Look for seed mixtures of Oriental vegetables, or make your own by combining packets of pak choi, Chinese cabbage, mizuna, mustards and green-in-the-snow	'William' (early September ripening), 'Concorde' (mid- to late September), 'Comice' (the best tasting pear – second week October)	**RECOMMENDED CULTIVARS**

← PEPPERS, SWEET AND CHILLI

Easy to grow with just a little protection.

Plants

Sweet peppers: six plants; chilli peppers: one plant

Plants will keep on producing fruits as long as you keep picking. Pinch out the flowers of sweet peppers towards the end of summer, as otherwise the existing fruit will not ripen.

Plant in your sunniest, most sheltered spot in May under cloches. Remove cloches when weather heats up. Provide lots of water.

Sweet peppers: don't bother with the basic pepper that can be bought in the shops but instead go for more interestingly shaped cultivars such as 'Corno de Toro' or 'Big Banana'.
Chilli peppers: 'Anaheim' (tasty), 'Thai Dragon' (very hot)

POTATOES, NEW →

Much more tasty and expensive to buy than maincrop potatoes. At their best when eaten fresh.

Seed potatoes

3kg (7lb) bag

Dig and eat as required

Get the potatoes into the ground as early as possible to get an early crop. In the south this will be in March, but you may need to cover the ground with fleece. Pre-chit the seed before planting (i.e. keep them in a light, cool but frost-free place from midwinter so that they can sprout). Plant with a few centimetres of soil covering them, 30cm (12in) apart. Earth up by regularly covering the top growth with soil as it appears, to prevent greening of potatoes and to protect from frost. When flowers appear, water well. Ready about seventy days after planting.

'Anya' (salad potato), 'Home Guard' (brilliant flavour), 'Epicure', 'Swift' (particularly early cultivar)

GOOD-VALUE ALLOTMENT CROPS

PLANT OR SEED?

HOW MUCH?

TIPS

GENERAL INFORMATION

RECOMMENDED CULTIVARS

RASPBERRIES →

Tasty and easy to grow.

Plants (known as canes)

Twelve plants

Autumn raspberries are the simplest to grow and start cropping as early as July, so do not bother with summer raspberries if space and time are limited

Plant canes in late autumn 38cm (15in) apart into well-prepared soil. Provide good, strong support and tie plants in as they grow. Water as fruits well. Harvest and eat as soon as mature. In December each year, cut the canes of autumn raspberries down to ground level. Prune summer raspberries in autumn; cut the fruited stems down to the ground, and tie in two new shoots horizontally, which will bear next year's fruit

'Joan J' (long cropping season), 'Autumn Bliss' (good flavour)

REDCURRANTS	RHUBARB	GOOD-VALUE ALLOTMENT CROPS
Very attractive plants when in full fruit. Ripe currants can be easily frozen for later use.	Easy to care for and delicious, as well as being the first fruit of the year.	
Plants	Plant	**PLANT OR SEED?**
Two plants	One plant or 'crown'	**HOW MUCH?**
For best-sized fruits, water when the fruit is swelling	Stems should always be 'pulled' rather than cut: pull the stems away from the crown using a twisting motion. For the best crops, follow blanching instructions. Do not to eat leaves, as they are poisonous	**TIPS**
Plant between autumn and early spring. Train plants into a fan shape against a wire frame, rather than as a freestanding bush, as this makes fruit easier to reach for picking and takes up less room. Prune in early spring; cut back new growth at end of each branch by half and remove any overcrowded, damaged or diseased branches.	Prepare soil well with well-rotted organic matter before planting from mid-autumn to early spring. Do not remove any stems during the first year. For the earliest and most tender stems, blanch or 'force' by placing a plastic bin with the bottom cut out over the plant in winter before the plant has started into growth. Fill with straw for extra warmth. Pull the stems as soon as they are a more than about 23cm (9in) long. Stop pulling around April and remove bin to give the plant a chance to recover for the rest of the year. Mulch with well-rotted manure and water well. Unforced plants can be harvested into summer	**GENERAL INFORMATION**
'Rovada', 'Red Nose'	'Champagne' (fine flavour), 'Stockbridge Arrow' (bright red sticks)	**RECOMMENDED CULTIVARS**

SHALLOTS	SPRING GREENS
As easy to grow as onions, but better, sweeter more interesting flavour. Also more expensive and hard to get hold of in shops.	Very rapid-growing looseleaf cabbage. Tasty and nutritious, and will stand all winter. Use shredded in stir-fries and salads.
Sets (small bulbs)	Plants
Twenty bulbs	Thirty plants
It is essential to keep weeds down	Pick as required throughout winter
Plant bulbs 20cm (8in) apart from midwinter to early spring in well-manured ground. Water well in March and April when just starting into growth. Lift when leaves start to turn yellow and leave to dry in a cool, dry place for about ten days. Store and eat as required	Each plant does not produce a huge amount, so plant relatively large numbers of plants across plot, 22cm (9in) apart, in July to eat from September onwards
'Golden Gourmet' (large bulbs, mild flavour), 'Eschalote Grise' (the best-flavoured, gourmet cultivar)	'Mastergreen', 'Wintergreen'

	← SPRING ONIONS	STRAWBERRIES	GOOD-VALUE ALLOTMENT CROPS
	Very easy-to-grow ingredient that adds interest to salads.	Particularly worth growing if you can get hold of the older cultivars, which are far tastier than the modern commercial ones.	
	Seed	Plants	PLANT OR SEED?
	2m (6ft) rows	Ten plants	HOW MUCH?
	Water well in dry conditions	Pick and eat as they mature	TIPS
	Direct sow each row thinly every four weeks from March to September for crop from late April to October. Make final sowing of a few rows to grow through winter	Plant out in April in two rows of five plants. Place straw closely around all the plants to keep the fruits off the mud once they appear. Keep well watered but do not wet the fruits or else they will rot. Pick fruits from the first year. Plants will need replacing after three years	GENERAL INFORMATION
	'White Lisbon' (mild flavour, use for summer and winter), 'Furio' (red onion, mild flavour)	'Royal Sovereign' and 'Garigette' (both fairly low yielding but particularly tasty older cultivars)	RECOMMENDED CULTIVARS

SPINACH	SQUASH →
Very easy-to-grow, cut-and-come-again crop, which is highly nutritious.	Takes up a lot of space, but really delicious, especially cut up and roasted. Unusual types are available that you will not find in the shops.
Seed	Plants
3m (10ft) rows	Two plants
Make sure that plants never dry out, as this can make them go to seed	Cure and store to eat when required
Direct sow each row every two months during growing season with the first sowing in March. Each plant can be cut, using scissors, several times before it is exhausted. Make last sowing in September and cover with a cloche for cropping throughout winter	Needs lots of feed and moisture. Dig planting pit and fill with well-rotted manure before covering the top with soil. Plant direct into hole as soon as frosts have passed. Water well throughout season. When mature, cure the fruits by cutting them off the plants, stem attached, and leaving them to dry in the sun for a week or so. Move indoors if wet weather or frost threaten
'Galaxy' (good for baby leaves for salads and larger leaves for cooking), 'Bloomsdale' (good flavour for summer crops), 'Triathlon' (for earliest crops)	For best value for space, go for cultivars that produce lots of small fruits, which can be eaten at one sitting, rather than just a couple of huge fruits: 'Squash Festival' (nutty-flavoured fruits can be baked whole), 'Baby Bear' (tasty orange flesh)

SWEET CORN →

A crop that is really at its best when eaten fresh, but it takes up a lot of space for the amount it produces, and may not mature well in cooler areas, so it is not for everyone.

Plants

Twenty plants

Harvest and eat as mature

Needs a sheltered spot and lots of moisture, so work well-rotted organic matter into the soil and water regularly in dry spells. Plant out as soon as frost has passed. For best pollination and crops plant in a 'grid' or 'block' formation with plants 45cm (18in) apart. Harvest as soon as the tassels start turning brown: test for ripeness by peeling back skin and seeing if kernels are yellow (rather than white) and juicy, and pick and eat as soon as ripe

Look for 'supersweet' cultivars: 'Indian Summer', 'Earlisweet', 'Swift'

PLANT OR SEED?

HOW MUCH?

TIPS

GENERAL INFORMATION

RECOMMENDED CULTIVARS

← TOMATOES	GOOD-VALUE ALLOTMENT CROPS
Taste so much better home-grown than bought that they are an allotment essential. Extremely versatile and tasty.	
Plants	**PLANT OR SEED?**
Ten plants	**HOW MUCH?**
Grow as many as ten different cultivars to give a variety of tastes, harvest times and uses. Pick and eat as mature	**TIPS**
Need sunny sheltered spot out of strong winds if possible. Buy nice strong plants and once frosts have passed plant out into ground rich in organic matter. Insert strong stake to support plants. Remove side shoots as plants grow and tie in regularly. Give plenty of water, particularly as the flowers are setting. Do not wet the leaves	**GENERAL INFORMATION**
Cherry: 'Supersweet 100', 'Cherry Belle', 'Sungold' Beefsteak and marmande: 'Black Russian', Super Marmande', 'Costoluto Fiorentino' Plum: 'Santa', 'Roma'	**RECOMMENDED CULTIVARS**

5

THE
FIRST
YEAR

The first year on your allotment is a critical time. You have enthusiasm on your side, but the majority of people who abandon their allotments do so within the first year. It is essential that you approach this crucial time with the right attitude. The most important thing to remember is that you can't do everything; give yourself a break and don't expect to win Best Plot this first year. There will be times when your plot looks messy, when it doesn't come up to the standard of those around you and when favourite crops fail to flourish. Don't beat yourself up about it.

TARGETS FOR YOUR FIRST YEAR

You need to be realistic about what you can do, and a good target to aim for is to get one-third of your plot weed free and planted up by the end of the year. Whatever size of plot you have, this should give you enough space to get plenty of salad crops and a few other bits and pieces out of it and make you feel like a proper allotment gardener, but one-third is still a small enough area to be attainable and easily kept under control once cleared. It will give you an area where you can practise your techniques before you start your onslaught on the whole plot.

So when is a good time to get started? For new allotment holders, particularly those with little experience of gardening, some time in mid-spring, perhaps April, is probably the best time. Horny old gardeners will tell you to get on to your

new plot and start digging in midwinter, and it is true that getting some land cleared then will give you a head start. But winter can be grim and off-putting, and there is little point in making life hard for yourself. In winter there is much time when the ground is wet and should not be worked because of the possibility of compacting it and ruining its structure. By April the weather is starting to warm up, and it is also much more pleasant to be outside; rather than dreading the cold and rain, you will find yourself longing to get up to your plot and out into the open air. In spring allotment sites become far more populated with allotment holders starting to cultivate, sow and plant, and you may find this extra company encouraging. Fellow gardeners are a wonderful source of information, and it is great to be able to see other people in action, and talk to them about how they do things.

Although it is important, in the long run, to grow your crops in different places each year as part of a rotation plan (more on this on page 102), the first year is not the time to worry about this. You will eventually have a series of beds in full cultivation that you can plant up with the correct type of plant, rotating each to a different bed the following year. However, this first year you will be desperate to get something into the ground and growing, and that is exactly what you should do. As soon as an area is clear of weeds, plant it up. Making a rough note of

Do not panic about getting things into the ground in early spring in your first year. Many vegetables, such as maincrop potatoes, will still crop from summer planting

where each crop went in the first year will be helpful when deciding what to plant where in subsequent years, but that is really as much as you need do about crop rotation for now.

You may think that a spring start will leave you with little time to grow crops in your first year. This is far from the case. There are many vegetables that you can put in from late spring onwards that will give you quick returns. French beans are wonderfully quick to mature, and you can put in maincrop potatoes to be dug up in autumn as late as June or July. Lettuce and carrots will germinate and mature quickly, and you can also put in tomato plants, bought from a garden centre, as soon as the risk of frost has passed.

You will pour much of your energy in your first year into getting the weeds under control, and April is the time when weeds start actively growing. It may surprise you, but this actually makes them easier to control; some are not even visible until they start growing, because they die down under the soil over winter, while most are hit harder by the various weed control methods once they have put on a bit of soft, lush growth. The sun and wind of a typical spring day is the perfect drying environment, and any weed roots that are exposed on such a day will be quickly desiccated and killed.

WEED CLEARANCE

When it comes to weed clearance methods, you reach a bit of a fork in the road and need to make a few decisions about how you want to run your plot. The two routes are organic and non-organic. This chapter will give you the methods to follow for each, as well as some tips as to how to go about each to make them as effective as possible. When it comes to using chemicals, this means giving you information on the best timings and techniques in order to get the maximum impact with the lowest possible usage, and in the case of organic methods, timings and techniques to make your hard work efficient and effective with the minimum backache and heartbreak.

There are pros and cons to each approach. Some chemical use will make your life much easier when it comes to weed control and control of certain pests. However, many people feel uneasy about using chemicals on their own produce. If you buy organic veg from the supermarket, you will probably want to produce crops that you know have not been sprayed. A third approach would be a compromise between the two: you might use herbicides to clear the patch initially, in order to get it under control in the minimum of time, and then switch to organic management from then on, so that no chemicals are directly used on your crops. Both non-organic and organic methods can be carried out within the half-hour allocation of time, but you will have to accept that a chemical approach will have an instant impact and achieve a quick clearance of the ground that is just not possible with an organic approach.

NON-ORGANIC WEED CLEARANCE METHODS

The most widely available chemical to use for weed clearance, if you are going down the non-organic route, is glyphosate. It is sold as Tumbleweed or Roundup. There are two reasons why it is considered particularly useful. The first is that is a translocated herbicide. This means that the active ingredient does not just kill whatever part of the plant is touches, as would be the case with a contact herbicide. It is actually taken into the weed's system and drawn down right into the roots, and so kills them as well as the top growth. The other main reason it is widely used is that it is said to break down on contact with soil, which means that there should be no residues there by the time you plant or sow your crops. However, there is currently considerable debate about its toxicity and its effect on the health of users, as well as its persistence in the soil. If you are at all concerned about chemical residues in your soil and on your fruit and veg, it is best to avoid chemicals altogether. Always follow the instructions for use as recommended by the supplier.

If you are going to spray, you will need to buy a knapsack sprayer or large hand-held sprayer (from a DIY shop or larger garden centre). Look for one with a sprinkler bar and fan nozzle jets. These produce a fine spray of the product that coats the weeds efficiently, allowing you to use less of the product. The sprinkler bar means that the chemical is released only when it is close to the ground, and this reduces the chances of it drifting on to other plots or areas where you do not want it. Some allotment societies may own this equipment and be prepared to loan it to plot holders. Some may even offer to spray new plots, in order to help new allotmenteers get off to a good start, so it is worth asking. You can mix the herbicide in a watering can and sprinkle it on to the plot using a watering can rose, but the droplets will be very large and so will not coat the leaves as efficiently, and you will also end up using much more of the product (which is more often than not quite expensive) than you really need, as water runs out of watering cans so quickly.

Before you start applying herbicide, you should have decided where your paths are going to be (see page 25). Mark them out and make sure that you avoid them when spraying; it is a waste of time to spray the grass off and then returf. The best time to spray is in mid- to late spring, when weeds are actively growing. The translocating action will be more effective than it would be if the weeds were dormant or just starting into growth, as the plants' systems are working at full pelt. The ideal day is one that is dry but not windy, as any breeze can cause a drift of the herbicide on to other plots. There is a possibility that glyphosate harms bees and other beneficial insects, so spray in the middle of the day, rather than in the morning or evening when they are at their most active.

NEXT PAGE A densely planted plot creates a good incentive to keep on weeding, and the crops act as competition for the weeds.

When spraying, be sure to wear protective gear, such as a facemask, gloves and an overall. It is a good idea to work backwards so that you do not walk over areas you have sprayed. Work systematically up and down in rows, and use markers at the end of each sweep so that you can see where you have sprayed and so do not overlap and apply excess product. Remove the boots you are wearing after spraying and before walking on any grass; otherwise you will get comedy footprints of dead grass across it. Have a shower after spraying and wash your clothes to get rid of any traces of the product.

You should make your first application in spring and then return to spray again about a month later. This will show up any patches that you have missed the first time round. If you have particularly persistent weeds it can be a good idea to spray them in autumn, just before they die down for winter. At this time those that die down for winter, such as Japanese knotweed, take stores of energy from the leaves down into the roots, and so an application of a translocated herbicide at this time will be taken right down to the heart of the plant.

ORGANIC METHODS OF WEED CLEARANCE

Organic methods of weed clearance are generally much more labour- and time-intensive, but they will at least leave you with the peace of mind of having used nothing but elbow grease to clear your plot. When attempting any of

these, it is a good idea to force yourself to stick to the half-hour system and do a little each day. You will see far more consistent results and will avoid putting your back out.

DIGGING OUT

The simplest, most backbreaking method is simply to dig the weeds out. It can be painfully slow if you want to do it really well, but it is pretty effective. Although it will get rid of most weeds, there will be some pernicious perennial weeds that you cannot get every last bit of: you will always end up leaving little bits of roots in the ground that will spring back into life. You should be prepared to come back and dig these up again.

TURNING THE SOIL

A combination of digging out the worst weeds and simply turning the rest of the plot over can be effective. By turning the soil you will expose the worst of the roots, allowing them to dry them out. If you have heavy soil, it will expose it to the elements, which help it to break down, and you will be able to come along at a later date and pick out many of the roots with the soil in a far more workable condition. Turning the soil just once is not enough, though: to clear the ground you will have to do it repeatedly, digging out all the roots of weeds as you go. For the best results, choose a spring day when there is sun and wind, which will cause the dug roots to dry out rapidly.

Back to basics: digging weeds out is hard work, but it is effective and completely organic

COVERING THE SOIL

Excluding light from the weeds will eventually kill them, and this can be achieved by placing a thick, light-excluding layer over the ground. First, you should strim over the whole area to cut the weeds down to a manageable size (you may be able to borrow a strimmer from a neighbour or from your allotment society, or you could try a tool hire shop). Try to dig out any large, woody weeds, such as brambles, which will prevent you from getting a good, flat surface. Once you have the area roughly cut and levelled, lay your light-excluding mulch. You will need to make a good job of this, making sure that every inch is well covered, as opportunistic weeds will seize upon any chinks of light. Ideally, you should leave this mulch on the ground until it kills all the weeds beneath it and they rot down into the soil.

Covering the soil with a light-excluding mulch is a slow but organic weed clearance method

The best material to use is cardboard, weighted down with stones, as it is thick enough to exclude light but relatively quick to decompose and disappear into the soil. If you find that weeds grow through the cardboard, you may need to add another layer. Alternatively you could use layers of newspaper, although these are harder to control, particularly when laying them. Black plastic is often used, as it forms a permanent barrier to light, but it makes an ideal hiding place for slugs and snails. Old carpets are good, as they are thick and heavy, but you should try to use all-wool ones, which may be quite hard to come by, as otherwise they will not get absorbed into the soil and you will be left with lots of half-rotted fibres and bits of underlay all over your plot. Carpets may contain toxins that could leach into the soil.

The main problem with the light-excluding method is the amount of time it takes. Killing the weeds will take at least a year, and two would be better. It can be carried out at any time of the year, usually the sooner you do it the better. However, if you are considering this method in late winter or early spring, wait until the weeds are actively growing. Many, particularly those that die down over winter such as bindweed, will have stored reserves of energy at the end of the previous summer to get them through the winter and early spring until they have put up enough growth to start photosynthesizing and supporting themselves again. If you can put the mulch down just after this first flush of growth, you will deprive them of this vital injection of solar energy just when they are at their most vulnerable.

REMOVING THE SURFACE OF THE SOIL

If your plot is covered almost entirely in couch grass, you might find it easiest simply to remove the top layer of turf and soil, and either stack it grass side down to exclude the light, or cover it with a light-suppressing cover. The couch grass will eventually die and rot down, and you will be left with a beautiful pile of topsoil and well-rotted organic matter to use on your plot. Removing the top layer will not remove all the roots, and you will have to dig the remainder out, but it will get rid of the worst of them and leave the rest exposed and easy to get at.

ROTOVATING

Some councils and allotment sites offer to lend a rotavator to help clear new sites, or will even come on to your plot and rotavate for you. A rotavator is a machine that has two circular blades that churn through the soil, slicing into it. It is used for 'clearing' plots because it has an instant impact: after a few hours' work you have what looks like a beautifully cleared plot. This is deceptive. If there are any perennial weeds at all in the soil, the rotavator will cut them up into many tiny pieces and spread these all over the plot. Pernicious weeds have earned their reputation because they are able to regenerate from the tiniest piece of root, and so all you do by cutting them up is propagate them and spread them around your plot. Added to this, frequent use of a rotavator can lead to soil compaction and problems with drainage.

Refuse all offers of rotavators until you are sure that you have got rid of all perennial weeds.

USING OTHER PLANTS TO KEEP THE WEEDS DOWN

Weeds get out of hand on abandoned plots partly because they have no competition. Simply planting other plants on your plot will help you to keep weeds under control. It is disheartening to clear an area and then return, a couple of weeks later, to find that it is covered in weeds and you have to start all over again. The best way to avoid this is to plant something in each spot as soon as you have cleared it. That way you will have more of an incentive to keep the area clear of weeds – you are more likely to pop back and hoe regularly while you wait for your seeds to germinate or your plants to get established than you are to bother to keep up a blank piece of land – and the weeds will have some competition.

If you do not have seeds or plants ready to go into your freshly cleared ground, consider sowing a green manure. Green manures are particularly useful if you have cleared some ground in autumn that you are not planning to plant up until spring, but they can be used any time you plan to leave a piece of ground bare for over six weeks. They are sold as 'green manures' but can be lupins, grazing rye, alfalfa, mustard, field beans or clover. Sown thickly over the ground, they germinate quickly and smother emerging weeds. They also help prevent erosion of soil nutrients and can even add nutrients to the soil. They are turned into the soil before they flower and set seed, and then left to rot down, so adding bulky organic matter, which helps to improve the structure of the soil.

If you have a particularly badly weedy piece of ground, removing the worst of the weeds and then planting it with potatoes (maincrop or new) can be a great way of clearing it. Any ground that is continually dug over will become progressively easier to work, and earthing up potatoes as they grow to prevent the new tubers from turning green in the sunlight achieves this. The simple action of turning the soil loosens weed roots from their hold and exposes them and the fact that it is repeated several times through the growing season seems to be enough to knock many weeds back. The large root systems of potatoes mean that much of the soil is broken up beyond what you have been turning. The following year you will find an area where potatoes have been planted to be the part of your plot that is the most weed free, with the most easily worked soil.

Other vegetables with particularly good weed-suppressing qualities include cabbages, pumpkins and courgettes. Their large leaves block out a huge amount of light over a long period of time and this prevents the weeds from thriving beneath them. The roots break the soil up well, and after cropping you will find the soil crumbly and in great condition.

Once you have cleared the ground, your soil may still need some attention before you start planting. There is more information on getting the best from your soil in chapter 6.

MANAGING YOUR 'FALLOW' AREA

You will be itching to get started on your cultivated third, where you can get plants in and start the more exciting side of allotmenting. However, getting a grip on your 'fallow' two-thirds is equally important. If you leave it in the state you find it, it will quickly turn into a messy, morale-sapping eyesore, with weeds that will set seed that drifts over your neighbours' plots. Weeds get worse and more deeply entrenched the longer you leave them, particularly perennials such as brambles, which will form a solid thicket that seems impossible to tackle.

If you are taking the chemical route, spray this area off when you spray the rest of the plot. Thereafter you will need to make extra occasional spot sprays in order to keep down weeds as their seeds drift on to this area, but you should not need to spray the whole area so thoroughly again, and your main problem should be annual rather than perennial weeds. If you are following an organic route, you can manage this rough two-thirds in different ways. You could remove the larger weeds and then strim the whole plot, before setting up a regular mowing regime as part of your half-hour timetable. Regular mowing is incredibly effective at killing most weeds; being cut down to the ground each time they are about to start a growth spurt can be fatal for all sorts of weeds, including docks, nettles, bracken and thistles. Eventually you will be left with an area of grass that is relatively easy to care for. Or you could use the year that you are going to let this area to lie fallow to your advantage and use the light-excluding method described on page 84. This will make the two-thirds much easier to clear once you are ready to start on it during your second year.

GETTING ALONG WITH YOUR NEIGHBOURS

One of the most daunting parts of getting started on a new plot can be your neighbours. Many people will be lucky and have supportive and encouraging allotmenteers on neighbouring plots. Even so, the sight of a perfectly manicured allotment on either side of yours can lower your morale, and some neighbours can be critical, particularly of slow progress.

The best advice, of course, is to ignore such intrusions and stick resolutely to your course, but this can be easier said than done. Be friendly to your neighbours, and ask their advice if you need it, but there may come a point when you have to keep your head down and get on with your work. Your neighbours may be concerned by your inexperience, but there is little anyone can say if they see that you are putting in regular hours, even if you only clear your plot slowly. If relations are good, tell them your plans. If they know that you are only trying to clear one-third in the first year, they won't see your slow but careful progress as a failure.

The one thing that will alienate you most from neighbouring plot holders is an overgrown weedy plot, and this is why the management of your fallow patch is of such importance. If you have cleared away any rubbish and are cutting your fallow patch regularly, they will have no reason to be concerned.

A final neighbour-impressing tip is to make sure that you always cut your grass paths and trim your edges. This is the nearest you can get to cheating: it is amazing the difference ten minutes' trimming can make, even if all within is utterly chaotic.

PACING YOURSELF

During the first year there will be so much to do that you may feel panicked, and as if you are not making progress. Resist any pressure to overdo it, either from your neighbours or from yourself. By sticking to half hour a day you will have time to do everything; you just have to have faith enough to resist throwing whole weekends at the problem. This may be your first time wielding heavy tools, and your body will need time to get used to it. Overdoing it will not help in the long run, as you are much more likely to get jaded.

Make a policy within this first year to do every job as well as you can. Rather than spending ten minutes whipping along your entire row of carrots but missing the tricky weeds growing in between them, spend the ten minutes on a third of a row, and weed it properly. It is cheering to know that you have done high-quality work and will not have to go back to that spot for some time.

6

NURTURING YOUR PLANTS

You may get great results at first simply by sowing or planting out direct into the soil and hoping for the best. But the time will come when some problem or other will hit you: the soil may be leaching nutrients, or your plants may get struck by frost or pushed over by the wind. You will make your allotment more productive and easier to manage if you learn how to nurture and care for your soil and crops.

TREATING THE SOIL

The soil is your greatest asset. You may find that the soil on your new allotment is incredibly fertile. This is particularly likely if it had been lying fallow for a while before you took it on, as it will have had time to recover from vegetables growing on it and removing all the nutrients. Equally, though, if you have inherited a plot that has been well used, the soil may be fairly exhausted, in which case it will need some treatment if you are to get the best from it. It will pay to spend some time getting to know your soil, and giving it some basic treatments, should that prove necessary – it nearly always does. Some basic amelioration can unlock the hidden potential of your soil, turning it from a lumpen mass that produces miserable crops to an easily worked, crumbly soil that produces prize-winning yields.

One of the things you should try to do early on is find out exactly what type of soil you have. This will affect the kinds of crops you can grow, and the level of success you can expect. There are also things that you can do, fairly easily, to make changes to the soil that will increase its workability and productivity.

Allotment soil can be dreadful. It has often been overworked, compacted and neglected over many generations and the result can be a ruined soil with an overly fine surface that becomes 'capped' in dry weather, which means that a fine layer of soil particles melds together, forming a layer over the soil that prevents water from penetrating. This is why it is sometimes better, despite the extra work involved, to go for a plot that has been abandoned for a while where at least the soil has had a chance to recover from intensive cropping.

You should be able to assess your soil's basic make-up just by digging it and getting your hands into it. The three main types are clay soil, silty soil and sandy soil. Most soils are a combination of these, and the physical and chemical properties of a soil depend on their relative proportions.

A soil that is predominantly made up of clay is heavy and holds a lot of moisture; you will find it almost impossible to dig after rain because of this. When you dig it, it will come out in big clods, and the spade may leave a shiny surface. Pick a bit up and feel it between your fingers. It will be smooth and cool to touch. It can be easily moulded and will hold its shape. A predominantly sandy soil is much easier to dig, and you will notice that water drains away very

Caring for your soil correctly can increase both the yield and the quality of your crops

quickly after rain. When you pick some up, it will feel gritty to touch, and it will not form into a ball. Soils that are made up mostly of silt particles feel silky when rubbed between the fingers and they retain moisture a little better than sandy soils. If you are very lucky you will have loam, which is a good balance of clay, sand and silt. This is easy to dig, crumbly, and drains and holds water well, and it forms into a soft ball that will disintegrate easily. It is, unfortunately, fairly rare.

There are benefits and drawbacks to each of these soils. Clay soil can be slow to warm up in spring, which delays sowing times, and it can be hard to work. However, it holds water and nutrients well, making it particularly fertile. Once plants are established you may not need to water, as there is always moisture available in the soil. It is a particularly good soil for growing plants that appreciate a good fertility, such as fruit trees and brassicas, but you will struggle to grow crops that need really good drainage, such as Mediterranean herbs, or those that need easy access through the soil, such as root crops. Sandy soils warm up quickly in spring but their free-draining nature means that nutrients are easily washed through and they can dry out more quickly than clay soils. Silty soils are vulnerable to compaction.

A pH test will let you know whether your crops could benefit from an application of lime

The good thing is that each type of soil needs much the same treatment to improve them. Lots of organic matter – in the form of well-rotted farmyard manure, garden compost or green manures – dug into any soil will improve its structure. Organic matter breaks up the dense, closely packed particles of clay soil, allowing small gaps where air can get in and water can drain out. But it coats the large, loose soil particles of sandy soil and knits them together, helping them to hold on to water and nutrients. Many forms of organic matter contain nutrients, but it is best not to rely on these to feed your plants and to use them primarily as a way of improving structure. That way you can dig them into the soil in autumn or winter, giving the weather and the worms time to work them well into the soil, without worrying about nutrients leaching out in winter rains. Never dig in fresh manure, as the ammonia in it can harm plants (and it smells horrible). If you are having manure delivered, ask how long it has been left to rot. If it is fresh, you will need to create an area on your plot where you can cover it and leave it for a year to mature before you start applying it to the soil. Alternatively, consider buying in bags of well-rotted manure. They will be much more expensive, but being easily moveable they have the advantage of allowing you to bring them in and apply the manure as and when you need it, so they do not use up precious allotment space over a long period of time.

It is essential to find out your soil's pH level early on. This may sound complicated and scientific but there are simple tests that you can buy from garden centres for just a few pounds. These tests usually comprise a solution that you add your own soil to. You then use a colour chart to match the colour of the solution to a pH level. It is a very simple test to carry out and will be a sound investment, as knowing the results can make a huge difference to your crops.

The pH of the soil is a measure on a scale of 0 to 14 of how acidic or alkaline it is. An acid soil will have a pH below 7, and an alkaline soil will have one above 7. Most vegetables grow best in a fairly neutral soil; the ideal is approximately 6.5, with anything between 5.7 and 6.8 being acceptable. The problem with an excessively high or low pH is that both can 'lock out' nutrients, so that even if nutrients are present in the soil in large quantities, plants can't access them and so do not grow as vigorously as they should. This will result in lower yields than you would hope to get on a pH neutral soil.

If your soil is too acidic (or the pH too low), this is pretty easy to remedy with applications of lime (see below). Making your soil less alkaline (by reducing the pH) is more tricky. If you find that the pH of your soil is too alkaline, the best thing to do is plant into it as it is, as most vegetables can tolerate a relatively high pH. The process of continuous cropping and cultivation, along with the chemical action of rain, will gradually lower the pH. Do not add mushroom composts to alkaline or neutral soils, as these products often contain chalk, which can lead to an increase in pH. Conversely, such composts would be useful on acidic soils.

Lime is sold in a powdered form, which is spread all over the soil before being roughly dug in. It is worth bypassing the small boxes sold in garden centres and heading for the allotment shop, if you have one. Such a shop will sell it by the hundredweight, and this is the sort of quantity in which you will need to apply it if it is to make any difference (it is incredibly cheap, even in these quantities). Apply it in spring, and then watch your crops grow to almost miraculous proportions as they unlock all the hidden potential in your soil. Lime is also a secret weapon in the war against clay soil, as it can help to break it down and make it more workable. You will need to repeat the whole exercise – pH test and liming – each year, as the pH level will gradually drop.

FEEDING

If your plot has been left fallow, you will probably find that there is little benefit in feeding your plants for the first year or so, but if it has been heavily cropped you may need to apply some fertilizer to the soil, to replace the nutrients removed by the previous crops. All fertilizers are made up of a combination of three main nutrients which plants need in large quantities, each of which encourages a particular type of growth. Nitrogen (N) is the nutrient that is most needed by most vegetables, and it encourages lots of leafy top growth. Phosphorus (P) is particularly good for encouraging root growth and potassium (K) for encouraging good flowering and fruit formation. All plants need a combination of these three nutrients, plus lots of micronutrients, to survive and grow well, but each needs them in varying quantities depending on the part of the plant (leaf, root or fruit) that is to be cropped. The abbreviations N, P and K are commonly used on fertilizer packaging, and the N:P:K ratio shows how much of each is present in the product.

You might think that you should buy specialist fertilizers for each crop, but in fact this is not necessary. As long as the soil is relatively fertile, only nitrogen is likely to be lacking, although you could consider applying a potassium-rich fertilizer for fruiting crops such as tomatoes and peppers. A general fertilizer that is high in nitrogen would do well by most crops, and the pelleted forms of chicken manure and seaweed that are widely available seem to be among the most effective at getting the nitrogen to the plants in a form that they can use. These can just be sprinkled around the crops (according to instructions on the packaging) at any time during the growing season. As I said before, many people believe

that the well-rotted manure they apply to the soil each autumn is a good fertilizer, but in fact the actual levels of nutrients it contains are relatively low and it is best used for soil improvement only.

Inorganic or artificial fertilizers, such as sulphate of ammonia or potash, or the general fertilizer Growmore, tend to be fast-acting. The nutrients reach the plant quickly, but the effect may be short-lived. Organic fertilizers, such as fish, blood and bone or pelleted chicken manure, often contain more micronutrients and act more slowly; they also promote the activity of beneficial soil organisms, such as bacteria, which are required to convert the fertilizer particles into a form that plants can absorb.

WATERING

Watering is a necessity on all allotments, but the amount you will need to do will vary dramatically depending on your soil and local climate. Plants grown on a clay soil in a damp part of the country may only need watering in when they are planted out or sown, while the same crop on a sandy soil in a dry area will need daily watering at certain times of the year.

Generally the more water you can give your crops, the better they will be. Even before the edible parts are formed, water will help the plants to grow large and healthy, and that will improve the quality and quantity of your crops. However, if time is short, with certain crops you can improve cropping most significantly by watering at particular stages of their development. This will usually be when the crop part of the plant is forming. Potato tubers form when the plants start flowering, so you should give the plants extra water then. With fruiting plants, such as raspberries, the key watering time is when the fruits are swelling. Lettuce, courgettes, sweet corns, melons, aubergines and French and runner beans benefit from lots of water, and should be watered as often as you can manage. Brassicas, on the other hand, don't really need watering once they are established, and will produce great crops without any extra input. Carrots also need very little extra watering once they have germinated.

There is a bit of a knack to watering; you can't just splash it around any old how, at any time. Well, you can, but if you do you will lose lots of water through evaporation, and you may do some damage to the plants. The best time to water is in the evening. At this time the temperature will be dropping and so the water is less likely to disappear into the atmosphere and more likely to end up getting right down to the roots of the plant. In summer you may need to leave watering as late as 7pm. Another reason to wait this late is the damage that the combination of heat and water can do to plant leaves: droplets that fall on leaves can heat up, particularly if they are in direct sunlight, and the heat can leave scorch marks. A final reason to water later during warm weather is that hauling a couple of watering cans around is less

exhausting in the cool of the evening than it is in the middle of the day.

The technique for watering all crops is the same: try to water the soil rather than the plant. Even in the evening water on leaves can be a problem, as it sits on the leaves and cools and may encourage moulds to form. Don't use a rose to water anything other than freshly sown seeds and seedlings (lettuces in particular will rot within a few days if you water all over their leaves with a rose). Get the spout as close to the base of the plant as you can. If you notice that water is just running off the surface of the soil, bank up a small amount of soil to create a circular ridge around the plant. This will prevent immediate run-off and keep the water in place long enough for it to soak down to the roots. The capillary action of moist soil makes it much easier to water than soil that has baked hard, so if you water every day you will probably get much less of a problem with water running off the surface, and need to use less water than you would if you watered less frequently.

You can reduce the amount of water you need to use by creating a 'dust mulch'. This is a technique used in the Mediterranean. It is particularly useful on clay soils, which crack in dry weather, creating large chasms down which water disappears and making it almost impossible to water efficiently. The idea is to create a fine tilth on the surface of the soil around the plants, and to maintain it with constant hoeing. Cracks never get the chance to form and watering is straightforward.

PROVIDING SUPPORT

Creating adequate support for your plants will prevent potential disasters. There is nothing worse than nurturing a plant all through the year and then finding that its flimsy support has collapsed at the crucial moment, ruining your entire crop.

Whenever you are planting tall crops, consider the direction of the prevailing wind before deciding in what direction the rows should run. (If you do not know in what direction your prevailing wind blows, ask other allotment holders, or even contact the met office.) Commercial growers always plant a couple of sacrificial rows on the windward side of their rows. These act as windbreaks for the rest of the plants but seldom produce high-quality fruit. On an allotment, you do not have the space to allow you that luxury, but you can bear the principle in mind. Planting the rows at right angles to the prevailing wind will mean that all the plants will receive its full force, and this will lead to poorer-quality crops and make it more likely that the supports will give way in sudden gusts. Instead, plant the rows so that they run in the same direction as the wind. This way the wind receives the minimum resistance and so is less likely to push the supports over; and only the last couple of plants on each row become 'sacrificial', rather than all of them.

There are two main categories of support: those that are for permanent plants and those for annuals. Those for permanent plants must be incredibly sturdy. Raspberries are a case in point. Their long, whippy growth can reach up to 7ft in height, and their leaves expand to create plenty of wind resistance. On an exposed plot this can be a lethal combination. Support for raspberries needs to be much more sturdy than you might at first imagine. These plants will be in the same spot for many years, so build the support to last. You can make a good start by getting hold of some good-quality tree stakes made of something solid and water resistant such as chestnut wood. Pine is no use, as it will quickly rot away. Position one at either end of your row and string strong wire between them, which the raspberries can be tied to as they grow. The same style of support can be used for cordon-grown redcurrants, blackcurrants and gooseberries.

You will need to construct temporary supports each year for crops such as climbing beans and peas. Permanent supports would be no good for these crops, as they would prevent you from using the ground after the crops were over and from moving the crop from place to place each year. The most commonly used support for climbing beans is a double row of bamboo canes, tied together at the top. This is as good a system as any, as long as it is done well. Buy the highest quality, thickest bamboo canes you can find, making sure that they are good and long, at least 2.5m (8ft). Push them into the ground about 38cm (15in) apart on

Spend time making sturdy supports for tall plants, even for temporary crops such as climbing beans

either side of the row, leaning towards each other. At each end of the row make a tripod of canes, to give the whole structure stability, and make another tripod in the middle of the row. Then join the whole thing together by placing more canes horizontally in the 'V' formed where the canes meet at the top, and tying them in at each point. String tied between all the canes lower down will provide extra stability and give climbing plants something to cling to.

Peas and mangetout are traditionally supported with pea sticks. These are twiggy branches, often cut from hazel, although they can be from any tree that has fine, twiggy growth. They are pushed into the ground next to the pea seedling, which then clambers up through the twigs. They are an excellent support as long as they are long enough to push firmly into the ground. If you do not have access to any suitable branches, a coarse piece of netting strung between two sturdy supports is very effective.

Tomatoes are usually supported with bamboo canes, which are woefully inadequate. As these plants often end up with many pounds of fruit hanging from them, they really need a sturdy stake. In this case pine will do, as the plants will not be left in the ground year on year.

PROVIDING PROTECTION FROM FROST

During the main growing season you will not have to consider frost protection, but if you

extend the season into early spring or autumn, you will run the risk of losing precious seedlings and young plants to frost, or frost damaging with the result that they take longer to crop or produce lower-quality vegetables.

There are some plants that you will need to plant out fairly early in the year, at a time when frosts may or may not have passed. Early potatoes are a good example. They are usually planted in April, when there is still a definite threat of cold snaps. In their case, soil is an effective insulation. The parts of the potato that are under the ground are unlikely to be affected by the light frosts of early spring, so if you earth up the soil as they grow, you should not have a problem. You will need to give other early crops more protection by covering the bed with a double layer of horticultural fleece or perforated clear plastic. Pin down the edges of the fleece by tucking them into a slit trench made by a spade. Straw, grass mowings and even old cabbage leaves can also be spread over the soil to similar effect, but this many not protect the growing tips of some plants.

Fleece is a good standby for emergency frost situations, as you can throw it over a plant within minutes if a frost is forecast and simply remove it the next day. It may look flimsy, but the protection it gives is just enough to keep off the worst effects of frost. It can be particularly useful with small fruit trees, many of which produce their blossom

OPPOSITE Plastic bottles cut in half and pushed into the ground can protect emerging and newly planted seedlings from frost early in the year. A hard frost can lose you an entire crop of fruit if it hits a tree when the blossom is out. If you have a fruit tree in blossom, keep an eye on weather forecasts and be prepared to run up to the allotment and cover it with fleece at short notice.

If you would like to be more proactive in your extension of the season, consider investing in some lightweight, moveable cloches. These are not cheap, but will be a great investment, and far easier to use than some Heath-Robinsonesque contraption made from skip finds. Buy a set of decent-sized ones, at least 45cm (18in) high, in order to get the full range of uses out of them. The main purpose of cloches is to give plants some protection over winter. Placed over the soil, they provide enough protection to allow crops such as spinach and carrots to keep actively growing, almost throughout winter. This means that rather than relying on the old, tough carrots that grew the previous season you can have young and relatively tender ones. They also provide the perfect spot for winter salad leaves. Used at the beginning of spring, they can bring back sowing times of a huge range of vegetables, as you can leave them on until the frosts have passed, and when you remove them the plants will already be well established and ready to take off. Another use is for more subtropical vegetables such as aubergines and melons during summer. These are not reliable out of doors, as they need higher temperatures than our climate usually

provides. A cloche provides that little extra heat that makes all the difference.

Plastic bottles, cut in half and pushed into the soil over individual plants, can be a good way of nursing young plants through early, frost-prone times. They keep frosts at bay and can deter slugs, but come with a caution: take care to remove them before the leaves touch the sides, as frost will burn any touching parts.

COMPOSTING

Composting is an essential part of allotmenting. Not only does it produce lots of organic matter with which to improve your soil, but it is also the best way of disposing of the huge amounts of green waste that are produced by the average allotment. At its simplest, composting means combining all your waste and leaving it to rot down, but there is a little more to it if you want to prevent it from turning into a gooey mess that sits for years without rotting down properly.

The first thing you need to consider is which compost bin to go for. Many councils supply plastic compost bins, and these are perfectly serviceable. If you are happy to spend some money, you can buy ones with openings at the base, which allow access to the rotted-down stuff while the stuff on the top is still fresh. There are also lots of recycled materials that can be put to great use as compost bins; four pallets nailed together makes one of the most effective. If you buy or make something that is mobile, you can move it each time a load of compost is ready. This way you just remove the structure, spread the compost over the nearby area, then move it to a new position, creating one extremely well composted area at a time.

Whether you make your own or buy something in, make sure that you get one that is generously sized and lets a little air in but is not too open. Some people use four stakes for the four corners, and just wrap chicken wire around them, but this lets in a little too much air and the heap will dry out too quickly. One of the best systems is a set of three wooden compost bins (bought or home-made makes no difference). The reason you need three is that it allows you to turn the compost from one bin to another, and this is one of the keys to producing good compost quickly. You start filling the second bin when the first is full, and use the spare one as space to turn the first into. Eventually you should get a constant supply of good compost.

So what are the secrets of composting? The trick is to get a good mix of ingredients. If you only put in grass clippings or soft, leafy material, the heap will soon get slimy. If it is all dry, woody material, the heap will not start to rot down at all. A combination of the two is perfect. If your heap is getting slimy and you have no dryer material to add, throw in some shredded or scrunched-up newspaper and stir the heap up to incorporate it. If it is too dry, water it and cover it with a lid or a piece of

Councils often sell basic plastic composters to allotmenteers. They work well and are light, so can be easily moved around

To produce compost with the best possible consistency, you must add a balanced mixture of materials to your heap

carpet to keep moisture in and help keep the heap warm. The smaller the pieces of waste are, the quicker they will rot down. The perfect solution is to shred all waste through a garden shredder before adding it to the heap, but if you do not have one, simply chop up any larger pieces. Constant turning of the heap not only speeds up the composting process but prevents your heap becoming a home to compost flies. These flies lay their eggs in the top layer of freshly added material, so if you cover the new additions with old, more rotted-down stuff, they will not get access to them and will be less of a problem.

There are a few things you should not add to your compost heap. Anything too woody, such as cabbage and broccoli stalks, will take too long to rot down, unless they are well shredded. You must avoid composting anything with any sign of disease. Composting onion

tops contaminated with white rot would result in your spreading white rot spores over the whole plot with the compost. Similarly, it is a good idea to avoid adding any potato tops, as these can contain potato blight spores. Never compost any parts of any perennial weeds. Many can re-sprout from even the tiniest piece, and you will end up spreading the weed across the plot when you next dig your compost into the soil. Tree leaves do not make good additions to a compost heap, as they take such a long time to rot down. If you have lots of them, it is best to make a separate leafmould bin for them. Leafmould makes a superb soil conditioner and mulch, and a bin for leafmould is simply a cage made of wire netting. Once the bin is filled up, just wait for the leaves to decompose.

ROTATION

Rotation is the practice of moving each group of crops from one area to another each year. This helps to prevent the diseases and pests of each crop from building up in the soil, as they would if that crop were grown year after year in the same area. You should aim for a minimum of a four-year rotation. This means that you will need four separate beds, and that each type of crop will not be grown in the same area for four years. The main groups of crops that are considered as part of a rotation plan are as follows: beans and peas, root crops (including potatoes), brassicas and onions.

There are all sorts of rules you can follow in order to decide which crops should follow which, but these are the finer points. If you can make sure that the same crop does not grow in the same place year on year, you are halfway to winning the battle. That said, the qualities and growth habits of each crop can be used to the advantage of the following crop, and so it can pay to bear these in mind when choosing an order for your rotation. For instance, peas and beans are very good at fixing nitrogen from the air. Nitrogen becomes concentrated in nodules in their roots, and if these are snipped off and dug into the soil when the plants have finished cropping, the nitrogen will become available to the next crop put into that ground. Brassicas are particularly heavy feeders, and so they make a good follow-on crop from peas and beans. Potatoes are good at clearing the ground of weeds, mainly because they are earthed up so regularly, but also because they are very leafy, and so shade out weeds. Seedlings that are tricky to weed, such as those of onions, are a good follow-on crop.

Each crop will benefit from slightly different soil treatment before it is sown or planted out. The area where brassicas are to be planted should be limed, as this helps to prevent club root. Brassicas may also benefit from an application of manure. Root crops such as carrots and parsnips should not be planted into areas that have been recently manured. This is because manure can have high levels of magnesium, which makes the roots fork.

Digging and growing potatoes clears weeds well and they should be followed by crops that are fiddly to weed, such as onions

Onions too should not go into freshly manured soil, as there is a link between fresh manure and white rot.

If you get any recurring disease or pest problems, extend your rotation cycle to make it as long as possible. Some diseases and pests can stay in the soil for many years, and so the longer you can make your rotation, the more chance you have of starving out your particular problem, even if you can only extend the rotation for the one problem crop.

You will notice that some commonly grown allotment crops, such as pumpkins, courgettes and salad crops, are not included in the above information on rotation. This is mainly because they do not have too many problems and can be fitted in wherever there is space among the other crops. As a precaution, however, it would be wise to avoid planting them in the same spot every year.

7

KEEPING ON TOP OF YOUR PLOT

You may have had lots of fun thinking about what plants to grow and planning your plot. Starting to clear it and putting in your first plantings is also exciting, as you start to see your new empire taking shape. But there comes a time when you have to get down to the boring stuff. Everyday maintenance is not the most fun part of having an allotment, but it is most probably the most important. If you can keep on top of the everyday jobs, you will avoid having to spend long weekends catching up with the weeding.

The best way to avoid the feast-and-famine approach to allotment tasks is to try to make the half hour you spend there each day an integral part of your daily routine. If you wait until you feel like popping up there, you will run out of enthusiasm at the first sign of bad weather or as soon as there is something good on the telly that you want to watch. One of the simplest ways of incorporating a half-hour regime into your life is to make it part of a daily commute. Make a decision to leave the house three-quarters of an hour earlier than usual, and you will catch the allotment at a magical, peaceful time and have the site almost entirely to yourself. Call in on your way home from work and you will have an opportunity to relax and de-stress from the problems you have faced in the day, and to avoid taking them and your frustrations home with you. If you work from home, are retired or your plot is near your place of work, do your half hour before you eat your lunch every day. Make it as routine as having a shower in the morning or catching the bus home at night, and it will cease to seem like a chore and just become a part of your everyday life. It will become a more and more enjoyable one as you get the plot more under your control.

THE BEST USE OF YOUR TIME AT THE ALLOTMENT

Once you have got into this routine, you need to teach yourself how to manage your half hour at the allotment. One of the most useful things you can do is to make decisions about the work you are going to do before you go to the plot. Making the decision the day before is even better. It gives you the chance to plan ahead and make sure that you have all the tools that you will need with you. You can lose so much time by wandering about the plot and checking out the various jobs that you could spend your time on. If you can plan your work ahead you will be able to go straight to that job and start, rather than walking around feeling overwhelmed.

There are two main approaches to managing your time at the plot, depending on the sort of jobs that need doing and their urgency. The first approach is to break down a large job and do it over several half hours. The second is to break your daily half hour down further, into ten-minute slots, and so fit three small jobs into your half hour. With both approaches, though, you should stick rigidly to your allotted half hour.

The first approach is most probably the one you will employ during the busy times, and when there are particularly large, urgent or daunting jobs to do. It is important not to be too ambitious about how long such jobs are going to take you. Planting out potatoes is a case in point. Saying 'I will plant out the potatoes in today's half hour' is not realistic. There are several elements to this job, each fairly time heavy and taxing to the muscles, and by overstretching yourself at the start you will only end up over-running your time and getting worn out, or leaving the job half done and getting dejected. Instead, dedicate your first half-hour session to roughly digging over the ground where the potatoes are going to go. This may even take two sessions. Don't even take the spuds with you to the allotment until this job is done. Use the following session for planting, and one a few weeks later for earthing up when the first growth appears. The job will have taken you three, or maybe even four sessions, but you will not have broken your back doing it, and will have reinforced your pattern of daily visits. Try to start thinking about all larger allotment jobs in this way. How can they be broken down into several distinct jobs, each amounting to one manageable session? Never think, 'I have to dig over a quarter of the plot'; instead think, 'I have to dig over two square metres (or yards) of the plot, each night, for a couple of weeks.'

The second approach, that of breaking the half hour down into shorter, ten-minute sessions, can be more useful when things calm down a little as autumn approaches, when you are keeping the allotment ticking over and the jobs to be done are less urgent. At times like these you may think there is little point in keeping up your daily visits, but in fact on any allotment there is always something that needs doing; by putting in the time during these periods you will make life easier for yourself when the big rushes come. By tackling a few small jobs each time you will keep your enthusiasm up, and you will be in intimate contact with all areas of your plot; you will know at all times which areas are getting weedy and which plants are not looking their best and might be suffering from some sort of problem.

PRIORITIZING AND PLANNING

There will be times of the year when the number of jobs that need doing seems overwhelming and you will not know where to start. You know that you have the potatoes to plant out and the carrots to sow and that the weeds are starting to get bad. It hasn't rained for a week and your edges are looking scruffy. Just remember that you can't do everything, and some things are going to have to get put to the end of the list. Try not to feel guilty about this. There is simply too much to do in some seasons – spring, in particular – for you to be on top of everything. But what should you do first?

The most important job at any time of year is picking and harvesting; this should always be a priority. This is a job that can easily get tacked on to the end of a long list of other jobs, as if it were incidental, and then rushed in order to fit

it in, but in fact you should expect it to be pretty time consuming, and even occasionally to take up the whole half hour, particularly in mid- and late summer. Bear in mind that the whole point of having an allotment is to have nice things to eat; you are not growing for the sake of growing. If you are letting crops go over, or are not picking them at their best, because you are so busy weeding and watering, there is really no point to all your hard work. So the first job every time you arrive at the allotment should be to decide what you want for dinner that evening and to pick it. If you do this every day, always picking just what you want for that night or the next, harvesting should always remain relatively manageable. The only exception to this rule is when you are picking salad leaves in hot weather, when it might be best to wait until the end of your half hour to prevent spoiling.

The second priority will be putting plants or seeds into the ground. Getting things planted or sown at the right time is really important, as you can easily miss your window of opportunity. Some things will never catch up if sown too late. But keeping track of what goes in when can be one of the trickiest jobs. If you buy plants by mail order, the company should send them through at the correct time for planting out, which takes some of the hassle and thought out of the whole thing. If you buy plants from a garden centre, though, you will not get this service. Yes, they should supply them at about the right time for planting out, but as you won't know what is in stock until you get to the garden centre, you will have no chance to plan ahead and get the ground and any necessary supports prepared.

The same goes with seeds. Each seed packet should have a guide to the best time for sowing, but it is easy to buy seeds, stick them in a drawer and miss your moment because you are busy doing other things. You must at least make a point, particularly in spring and the height of summer, of getting your seed packets out every week and checking which seeds need to be sown in the next couple of weeks. A better idea might be to set up a card index system at the beginning of the year, when your seeds arrive. Make cards for each week of the year and put each seed packet into the week it needs sowing; you can split seed

ABOVE Make harvesting first on your list of jobs or else it can get overlooked, leaving you with crops that are past their peak

RIGHT The second priority should always be sowing or planting, so as to ensure a continuity of crops

packets for crops that need to be sown successfully. Using the information in the table in chapter 4, you could also put in reminders for when you need to buy vegetable plants from the garden centre. Another approach would be simply to set up an allotment calendar at the beginning of the year with all the timings already written on it, and to check it at the beginning of each week.

The jobs with the next highest priority are those that have an impact on the quality of the crops you are growing. These include weeding and watering. Weeding directly around the plants obviously gets higher priority than weeding around the edges of beds or clearing areas that are not currently planted up, as weeds compete directly with crops for water, food and sunlight, and so will reduce the size and quality of your crop if they are left to grow. This is particularly the case with members of the allium family – onions, spring onions, garlic – which are all particularly sensitive to competition from weeds.

The need for watering will change with the seasons and even daily, as weather conditions change. Plants that are currently flowering or that have fruit forming should have top priority within the watering hierarchy, as watering at these times will have a great impact on the quality and quantity of the crop. After these, any other plants that are obviously suffering from a lack of water should be next on the list.

Those jobs that are more concerned with the upkeep of the plot and the soil come last. It is obviously very important to manure the ground occasionally to keep the soil in good condition, but this is never really an urgent job. It will not have too much impact on the plants if you delay it, even by a few weeks. The same goes for edging and mowing. They are important jobs, especially if fellow allotmenteers or the allotment committee are putting pressure on you, but they will not directly affect the plants. However, one of the worst sights you can be greeted with on arrival at your plot is the paths all grown up to a foot and the unplanted beds all covered in weeds, so you will make yourself happier if you put by a little time each week to weed, mow and edge at least a small area.

In an ideal world you should, of course, aim to have no weeds on your plot at any time, but in reality this is impossible. In fact there is even an order of priority among weeds. First on the list are those that are growing near and among crops. Following at a close second are the perennial weeds. These must be taken out at the earliest possibility, as they will spread, either by underground root or by overground shoot, and become more of a problem the more grace they are given. Next come the annual weeds. These move swiftly up the order of priority, even perhaps into the top spot, when flowering threatens. Weeds have very quick life cycles and flowering means that they will be setting seed soon, perhaps even the next day. If that happens, you will end up with an escalating weed problem, rather than gradually eliminating them, as is the aim.

HOW TO – A GUIDE TO A FEW BASIC JOBS

DIGGING

It is often a good idea to completely dig over beds that have become compacted or that have been recently cropped. It helps to improve the structure of the soil and so enables plants to get their roots down into it more easily. Digging is particularly useful when carried out in autumn and winter, particularly on heavy soils. The reason for this timing is that, if the soil is dug roughly and left in large clods, frost and rain work upon it over winter and it can often become more manageable as a result. This is also a good time to add compost or well-rotted manure to the soil, as it becomes worked in over winter.

You may think that you don't need to learn how to dig – and it is indeed a fairly straightforward activity – but there are a couple of techniques that you might find helpful. You can just lift, turn and chop up each clod, but single digging is a more methodical approach that makes it easier to add organic matter. Decide on the area to be dug and lay a tarpaulin or large sheet of polythene at one end. Dig out a trench one to spade's depth, placing the soil on to the tarpaulin. Put organic matter such as compost or well-rotted manure into the bottom of the trench, and then dig a new trench alongside the one you have just dug, turning the soil from it into the first trench. Chop up the soil in the first trench,

mixing it with the organic matter. Continue digging trenches in this way and you will progress along your designated area. When you reach the end, you will be left with a trench but no soil to fill it. Pull the tarpaulin of soil around from the other end and put it into this last trench.

Double digging is a similar technique in which you dig down to two spades' depths. This is only really necessary if you have got a problem with soil compaction, which is often the result of frequently using a rotovator. This can result in poor drainage.

CREATING A FINE TILTH

When you sow seeds it is important to create a fine tilth of soil. This means breaking the soil down into small particles so that the seeds will be in constant contact with some soil. This prevents them from getting dried out, as they might if they fell between large clods of earth, and it provides the best conditions for germination. In order to prepare soil in this way you will first need to dig over the soil thoroughly. You might then use a fork to break up large clods, and could then leave the soil for a week or so to break down further. Once you've done this, you start to work on it using a rake. Rake over the surface and then use the end of the rake to tamp down any lumps of soil, before raking again. Continue this process until you have a fine, even surface.

NEXT PAGE For the most thorough results, work organic matter into the soil using the methodical single-dig system

111

SAMPLE WORK PROGRAMMES FOR EACH SEASON	SPRING
	In spring there is some picking to do, but the main work is getting plants and seeds into the ground. This is a very busy time for sowing and planting, so to get the timing right make these jobs a priority. Grass and weeds are growing apace, but it is hard to keep on top of them because of the other work that needs to be done first. I make sure that I put time aside, even at this hectic time of year, to do at least a little weeding, mowing and edging every week, to prevent the plot from ever getting too overgrown and out of hand.
MONDAY	Monday: put runner bean poles up in preparation for planting (full half hour)
TUESDAY	Tuesday: sow runner beans (10 minutes), sow carrots (10 minutes), start digging over the ground from where overwintered cabbages have been cleared (10 minutes)
WEDNESDAY	Wednesday: earth up potatoes (half hour)
THURSDAY	Thursday: sow salad leaves (10 minutes), tie in growing raspberry canes (10 minutes), mow a path (10 minutes)
FRIDAY	Friday: edge 5m (15ft) of paths (10 minutes), plant out tomatoes (10 minutes), weed (10 minutes)

SUMMER	AUTUMN	WINTER
In summer there is still some planting to do, but there is much more harvesting than earlier. Watering may become a higher priority, particularly if the weather is dry. Weeds need constant attention if they are not to become a problem, and I make sure that I allow no weeds to get to flowering and seed setting stage. When the weather is drier, the grass grows slower than it did earlier in the year, but paths and edges still need constant attention if they are not to get overgrown.	By autumn it is all about harvesting, and I have much more time for general upkeep of the allotment than I did in spring. I start to think about how the plants are going to survive the winter, and put up protection if it is necessary. Watering is less of an issue now, particularly if there is plenty of rain. Grass and weeds are still growing, but not at the rate they were earlier in the year.	In winter there is harvesting still to be done and a little planting, but the general care of the allotment – weeding, watering, edging – that has taken up so much of my time over the growing season has almost ended. It is a time to look at the plot's infrastructure, to consider any changes and to implement them, and consider what to grow the following year. It is important not to walk on or work wet soil, as you can ruin its structure. At these times there are other jobs I can be doing, such as looking at catalogues and ordering seeds.
Monday: dig early potatoes (10 minutes), plant out leeks (10 minutes), water (10 minutes)	Monday: pick autumn raspberries (10 minutes), sow green manure on bare ground (10 minutes), cover salad leaves with cloches (10 minutes)	Monday: harvest kale (10 minutes), prepare land for garlic planting (20 minutes)
Tuesday: pick gooseberries (10 minutes), weed around carrots (10 minutes), edge 5m (15ft) of path (10 minutes)	Tuesday: net brassicas to protect from pigeons (20 minutes), harvest beans (10 minutes)	Tuesday: look at seed catalogues and order seeds (half hour)
Wednesday: harvest courgettes (10 minutes), plant out cauliflowers (10 minutes), water (10 minutes),	Wednesday: weed (10 minutes), prune soft fruit bushes (20 minutes)	Wednesday: paint shed, making shed repairs (half hour)
Thursday: harvest French beans (10 minutes), harvest salad leaves (10 minutes), mow 5m (15ft) of path (10 minutes)	Thursday: harvest salad leaves (10 minutes), cut down summer raspberry canes and tie in new canes (20 minutes)	Thursday: harvest leeks (10 minutes), plant out garlic (10 minutes), plant broad beans (10 minutes)
Friday: hoe (10 minutes), water (10 minutes), mow 5m (15ft) of path (10 minutes)	Friday: harvest apples (10 minutes), make final cut of path edges (10 minutes), do final mow of paths (10 minutes)	Friday: harvest Brussels sprouts (10 minutes), roughly dig cleared area (20 minutes)

HOEING

Hoeing only chops the heads of weeds off and doesn't affect the roots at all. Because of this it is most effective on annual weeds, which will usually be killed by this treatment, and is less so on perennial weeds, the roots of which will sprout again. Choose a hot, dry or windy day on which to hoe. In these conditions, the top growth that you chop off and any roots that are pulled up quickly become desiccated and die. In damp conditions there is always the possibility of them taking root. Take the hoe and slide it along the ground, just underneath the surface. The action should be quick and sharp, rather than slow, as the aim is to cut weeds rather than to pull them out. Take extra care near crop plants to make sure that you don't accidentally chop the tops off these, or damage the stems.

HAND WEEDING

Hand weeding is most useful around plants such as alliums that are grown fairly close together and where there is no space to run a hoe. It can consist simply of pulling up the weeds around the plants, particularly if they are annual weeds, or you can use a hand fork to dig out the roots of perennial weeds. It is important to remove as much of the root as you can, as any small amount left in the soil will sprout again.

Using quick, sharp movements, push the hoe beneath the surface of the soil, severing root from shoot

8

MANAGING PESTS AND DISEASES

Pests and diseases can have a devastating effect on an allotment. They can cause havoc among your vegetables, reducing yields and ruining quality. They are also disheartening, particularly when they affect crops that are almost ready to harvest. It is particularly depressing to have been eagerly eyeing up a crop, patiently waiting for it to reach prime ripeness, only to turn up on the allotted harvest day to find that birds and wasps have beaten you to it.

Many old-school allotmenteers swear by chemical controls for pests and diseases. In the short term, they can certainly cut down the amount of time you spend tackling problems. However, as laws on pesticide use become more stringent there are fewer chemicals available to the home or allotment gardener to control pests and diseases. Club root of brassicas and onion downy mildew are two common disease problems for which there is no effective chemical control for home use. Those chemicals that are still available are often not particularly effective and you may end up making multiple applications simply because the only product available to you just doesn't work all that well. In any case, you may wish to avoid the use of synthetic chemicals.

It can be simpler and, in the long run, less time consuming to take a more holistic approach to pest and disease control. The most important factor in keeping problems at bay is to get your plants growing strongly. Pests and diseases are far more likely to attack plants that are already stressed than those that are growing well and have all their natural defences about them. Be aware, though, that you may have to put up with more pest damage if you choose to take the organic route.

Soil is the key to growing strong plants. If plants can't get their roots properly down into the soil because it is compacted, if they meet waterlogging, or if they cannot extract enough nutrients or water from the soil, they get stressed and become more vulnerable to attack. A good system of rotation is essential, so that pests and diseases never get a chance to really get a foothold in one area. If you have been digging your soil over, improving it with organic matter, feeding it and adjusting its acidity or alkalinity according to the needs of your vegetables and rotating crops, you cannot help having good, healthy plants, and this will give you a serious head start on their attackers. You want to reach the stage where you have to put the minimum amount of effort into controlling pests and diseases.

However, some problems will sneak past even the best plant defences and for these there are other approaches to complement hearty growth. Take some time to experiment with a few different ways in which to reduce the damage caused by pests and diseases, to see what works best for you. By getting a good balance of all of these methods you will develop a plot that has its own balance of predators and pests, and this will allow you to spend less time on each individual problem.

RESISTANT CULTIVARS

One of the greatest weapons in the fight against pests and diseases is the use of resistant cultivars. These plants have been specifically bred to resist attack by particular pests or diseases. They are no guarantee, but chances are that if a pest is given a choice between a resistant cultivar and an ordinary one, the resistant cultivar will fare best. A few examples are: root-aphid resistant lettuces – 'Little Gem', 'Barcelona', 'Avon Crisp'; blight-resistant tomatoes – 'Ferline'; blight-resistant potatoes – 'Sarpo', 'Cara', 'Lady Balfour'; slug-resistant potatoes – 'Accent', 'Foremost', 'Kestrel', 'Sante'; carrot-fly-resistant carrots – 'Resistafly', 'Fly Away'; leaf-spot-resistant Brussels sprouts – 'Braveheart', 'Cavalier'; rust-resistant leeks 'Conora'. If you have a recurrent problem with a particular pest or disease, try to track down a cultivar that promises some resistance to it.

COMPANION PLANTING

There are many different reasons for companion planting. The most common are to confuse pests in one way or another, and to encourage beneficial insects, which may predate on garden pests. Planting crops in large monocultures, as commercial farmers do, suits pests and diseases perfectly. Pests can munch their way happily from one plant to another, produce young knowing that they will have immediate access to their favourite food,

and generally make themselves at home and start building up their numbers. The simple act of mixing your crops with any kind of flower throws them into confusion. At the very least, they have to use up a little energy hunting for their food rather than just stumbling into it.

Many pests find their favourite crops by smell. They will drift around fairly aimlessly until they get a whiff of, say, cabbage and then zero in on their prey. One of the simplest ways to confuse them, therefore, is by planting strong-smelling plants next to susceptible ones. Some of the most useful strong-smelling plants are those belonging to the allium (onion) family. Spring onions sown among carrots – either mixed in as part of the same row or in an adjacent row – may reduce attacks by the dreaded carrot fly, which tracks carrots down by the scent of their foliage and then lays its eggs in the soil near the carrot plants. It is also important to avoid crushing carrot foliage if possible, as this makes the smell stronger. When thinning, do not leave any bits of foliage lying around, and finish off by mounding up a little soil over the remaining carrots, as this provides a barrier that keeps the inevitable post-thinning visitors from getting to the roots.

If you are sowing your own seedlings (see chapter 10), alliums can also be used to ward off cabbage root fly. When you place a seed of your chosen brassica into the module of potting compost, drop one or two seeds of garlic chives (*Allium tuberosum*) in with it. The seeds will germinate at roughly the same time, and the smell of the garlic chives will mask the cabbage smell that the flies use for navigation, at a time when the brassica is at its most vulnerable. Alliums are also said to have beneficial antibacterial and antifungal properties, and so it may be worth mixing some in with any plants that are susceptible to rots.

Other particularly effective smelly plants include French marigolds (*Tagetes patula*), which will throw aphids and whitefly off the scent of all sorts of plants, including tomatoes. Choose the ones with the stinkiest leaves and plant them all over your plot. All the strong-smelling herbs make great companion plants, particularly camomile (*Chamaemelum nobile*), feverfew (*Tanacetum parthenium*), lavender and thyme, and it is a good idea to plant a few of these throughout your plot at intervals, just to scent the air.

Another reason for companion planting is that sometimes plants can derive some benefit from each other's growth habit, and so grow more lustily in each other's company. A classic example is that of sweet corn, beans and squash. These were traditionally grown together by American Indians because the squash covered the soil, suppressing weed growth and keeping it cool and moist, and the beans could use the sweet corn plants as support and climb up them. Potatoes and sweet corn also grow well together, as potatoes are good weed suppressors and, because of their differing habits, the plants do not compete for the same areas of soil and air. Lettuce grows well on the north side of tall plants such as runner beans, as

they quickly go to flower in heat and so benefit from the shade. Again, the simple act of growing these plants in among each other, or in alternate rows rather than in large blocks, will lead to fewer pest problems.

Sometimes companion plants can be used as sacrificial or lure plants to tempt pests away from edibles. Nasturtium (*Tropaeolum majus*) is an example. Grown close to any bean plant it will become covered in blackfly that would otherwise swarm over the stems of the beans. Squash the blackfly on the plant with your hands, if you are not squeamish, or remove the worst-infested pieces of the plant and drop them into a soapy or salty solution to kill the pests.

As mentioned earlier, a popular use for companion planting is to bring in beneficial insects which pollinate crops and can predate on garden pests. Different flowers attract different insects, so grow a range of companion plants if you can, to suit all tastes. Sage (*Salvia officinalis*), marjoram (*Origanum*), nasturtiums (*Tropaeolum majus*) and foxgloves (*Digitalis*) all attract bees; sedums, mint (*Mentha*), lavender and sweet Williams (*Dianthus barbatus*) attract butterflies; and cornflowers (*Centaurea cyanus*), yarrow (*Achillea*), coriander (*Coriandrum sativum*), fennel (*Foeniculum vulgare*) and sweet alyssum (*Lobularia maritima*) are favoured by hoverflies and lacewings. Poached egg plants (*Limnanthes douglasii*) and all kitchen herbs are good at attracting pollinators, which will improve the yield on fruit plants and vegetables such as beans and marrows.

PHYSICAL PROTECTION

Sometimes the simplest way of keeping pests off plants is to erect a physical barrier that they cannot get past. Horticultural fleece is often the best material for this. It is lightweight and so can be draped directly over plants, yet forms an impenetrable barrier. You may be concerned that it will stop light from getting to the plants, and so slow growth, but in fact the light that gets through is reflected back off the lower surface of the fleece, and bounces on to the plants. It can even increase the amount of light the plants receive. Used in this way it can completely stop aphids, carrot fly, cabbage root fly and many other pests from getting at your plants.

A fine mesh prevents the cabbage white butterfly from laying its eggs on brassicas

It is also a good idea to consider fleece for the period when top and soft fruits start to ripen. They can be devastated by birds and wasps just as they are reaching their ripest and tastiest. Simply draping a large piece of fleece over your strawberry bed or apple tree and then pinning or tying it down will make it more difficult for these creatures to reach your precious crops. Fleece is usually best used as a temporary measure for when pests are most active at the beginning of summer or for keeping your fruit safe. This is because water may have some trouble penetrating it, or conversely, you may get a build-up of weeds and warm moist air underneath it, which will provide ideal conditions for moulds and rots to set in.

If you have the time and money to set up a proper fruit cage, this will provide good protection from the attentions of birds at harvest time. A fruit cage is a large cage that is built over all your fruit trees and fruit bushes, and has a door in one side for you to gain access. It is covered in a mesh that will keep out birds but not pollinating insects. Fruit cages are better than draping the trees in fleece because they are permanent and easy to use once set up. This avoids the possibility of forgetting to cover the plants, or leaving it a little too late to do so. It also looks much better than mounds of fleece.

Brassicas suffer from the attentions of several pests, some of the worst of which are the cabbage white butterflies, which lay their eggs on the leaves. The eggs hatch and the caterpillars feed on the leaves. By erecting a structure of bamboo canes, hazel rods or wire hoops over the brassicas and covering this with a fine mesh you will keep the butterflies off and avoid the problem. A mesh will also exclude pigeons and other birds, which can occasionally attack brassicas. This may also suit other crops that might be attacked by birds, such as mangetout, sweet corn and soft fruits.

Companion planting can discourage cabbage root fly, as mentioned earlier, but a more conventional way is to use stem collars. Cabbage root fly lay their eggs at the base of the plant's stem, and the larvae then burrow down into the root. By placing a collar around the base of the plant – a 10cm (4in) disc of carpet underlay, roofing felt or cardboard with a slit cut in it – you prevent the fly from getting access to the roots and so prevent the problem from occurring. You can buy ready-made brassica collars from good garden centres.

Carrot fly can be confused by companion planting, but there is a complementary physical barrier that should keep them away from your carrots completely. Strange as it may sound, carrot fly almost always flies about 12cm (5in) off the ground. This is their best position for smelling their quarry. When they reach a barrier that is higher than this, they will just fly around it. You can use this fact to your advantage by placing a 23cm (9in) board, or some other impenetrable structure of the same height, around your row of carrots. They will have no way of getting at them. This also works with pots; if you want to grow carrots in a container, choose one that is at least 23cm (9in) high and the carrot fly will not trouble you.

If you have problems with aphids and notice that there are often ants around them on your plants, it is likely that the ants are 'farming' the aphids. Aphids excrete honeydew, which contains undigested sugars, and this is useful food for ants. To protect their food source, ants

will look after aphids, protecting them from predators and moving the fairly immobile pests around your plants to find more sappy and vulnerable parts. Stopping the ants from doing this will not wipe out your aphid infestation, but it will leave the aphids more vulnerable to predators. One way of preventing ants from getting to them is with a barrier of non-drying glue. This can be applied around the trunk of the affected plant, and will stop ants from travelling back and forth to their charges.

Another use for this glue is as a barrier to a pest called the winter moth. This attacks apples, pears, cherries and plums by laying its eggs near the buds in winter. In spring the larvae eat the buds, blossom and developing fruitlets. A band of non-drying glue or horticultural grease applied to the trunk in autumn will stop the females from crawling up the trunk to lay their eggs. The band should be applied about 1m (3ft) above soil level and be approximately 10cm (4in) wide.

Slugs and snails can be devastating, particularly early in the year, and they are among the hardest pests to control well. Slug pellets are effective, but they may be harmful to other creatures that might eat them, and to those, such as hedgehogs, that might eat slugs that have eaten them. If applied precisely as per the manufacturer's directions – in other words sprinkled evenly but very thinly – they are relatively harmless. Biological controls can be

Where pigeons are a problem, keep them off favoured crops by erecting strong structures covered in chicken wire

very effective against slugs, but not snails (see page 127).

You may find that barrier methods work. It is certainly a good idea to try every available method against them, as no method works alone. Try covering young plants completely with small cloches, such as a plastic bottle that has had the base cut out of it and is pushed down into the earth to prevent slugs from reaching the plant. This can be effective, but the plant will soon outgrow the space available and the cloche will have to be removed if it is not to be detrimental to the plant. Another method is to place a ring around the plant made of something slugs and snails are reluctant to cross. This could be a sharp material, such as gravel or cockleshells, or it could be a mat or a ring made of copper, which gives off a slight electrical charge that slugs and snails are supposed to dislike. This method can be fiddly and is also of questionable efficacy; sometimes, particularly in wet weather, slime trails will show that the slugs have simply clambered over your sharpest weaponry.

Another method that is worth trying with slugs is a beer trap. This involves placing a small receptacle of beer near vulnerable plants. Slugs are attracted to the smell of the beer, crawl in and drown. You need to cover the beer trap so that the beer is not watered down with rainwater. Make sure that the opening is high up enough that other creatures do not drop in, and the slugs have to actively crawl in. An old plastic milk container with a small amount of beer in the bottom buried into the ground a few centimetres (1in), with a hole cut about 5cm (2in) above the surface of the soil, makes an ideal trap. Alternatively you can buy ready-made traps. This method does collect plenty of slug bodies, but it is pretty gruesome.

You could also try scattering cut leaves of lettuce or weed seedlings near your plants. Slugs are supposed to prefer wilting vegetation to that which is actively growing, so the idea is that they fill themselves up on your wilted offerings and leave your plants alone. Obviously this has the disadvantage that you are actively feeding them up and so are encouraging a growth in the slug population, which could come back to haunt you when you forget to put out any cut leaves. It is worth trying in addition to other methods, however.

TIMING

Sometimes it is possible to avoid pests by sowing seeds at specific times of year. One example is broad beans. They almost always become completely covered in blackfly in spring. This is particularly a problem if you have sown them in early spring, because the top growth is soft and sappy and therefore more vulnerable to attack. However, by sowing suitable cultivars in late autumn or winter, the seeds germinate early and then toughen up over winter. They get a head start in spring, and have often flowered by the time the worst of the blackfly attacks begin. They also have tougher, less susceptible growth. If the plants have flowered before the blackfly starts to attack, it is much easier to control the pest. Blackfly always colonize the growing point of the plant, and you can pinch this out without affecting the flowers or developing bean pods.

Timing is also important in carrot growing. Carrot flies only lay eggs at certain times of the year, and so by timing your sowings you can make sure that no carrots are at a vulnerable stage at those times. Unprotected sowings can be carried out from mid-February to mid-April, from the beginning of June to mid-July and from the beginning of September to the end of October. You can still make sowings at other times, but if you do, use one of the protection methods given above, or cover the whole bed in fleece until the seedlings are at a less vulnerable stage.

BIOLOGICAL CONTROL

The development of biological controls that you can buy and apply to your allotment is fantastic for the half-hour allotmenteer. These controls are entirely natural and organic, and are safe to use around wildlife, pets or children. Their application generally just involves watering or sprinkling a pre-prepared pack of nematodes or other creatures on to the soil or directly on to the affected plants. In return you get several

Slug pellets are effective but may harm wildlife. There are several organic alternatives that are worth trying

weeks of control (at the very least) without having to do anything else. They are expensive, but if you are prepared to spend the money they can be extremely effective.

One of the best-known biological controls is for slugs. A nematode that preys on slugs occurs naturally in the soil, but not in the sort of numbers required to keep them under control and prevent them from making a mess of your plants. These nematodes can be bought in the form of a product called 'Nemaslug', which you add to water and then sprinkle over the soil, so boosting numbers. You will need to make several applications to keep the slug population down throughout the growing season, but the control is extremely effective. It can be applied from mid-March until October outdoors, or at any time of the year under glass. It is a good idea to start early, especially if you are planting out young, tender seedlings, of which slugs are particularly fond. As it is a naturally occurring slug predator it does no harm to any other wildlife, even those that might eat the dying slugs after they have been infected with the nematodes.

The larvae of lacewings and ladybirds are fantastic at controlling aphids. You can try to attract them by using companion planting (see page 121), but if you still suffer from high populations of aphids, it is possible to buy in reinforcements. Lacewings are bought as larvae and sprinkled directly on to affected plants. These larvae munch through the aphids,

before turning into adults. These adults then lay more eggs, often among aphid colonies, which will emerge as carnivorous larvae. Both ladybird adults and larvae eat lots of aphids. They can be bought as larvae and, again, sprinkled directly on to affected plants. Adult ladybirds will lay eggs and the larvae hatch out and help with control. Many suppliers offer for sale ladybird and lacewing houses or boxes, but as there is no shortage of naturally occurring overwintering sites for these insects, such purchases may not be necessary.

It is in polytunnels and greenhouses, where pests can thrive in the warm conditions, that biological controls work best, as the enclosed environment means that the predators and parasites are less likely to wander elsewhere. The two most common problems are glasshouse whitefly and glasshouse red spider mite. The former is controlled by a parasitic wasp, *Encarsia formosa*, which lays its eggs in the whitefly's scale-like nymphs. Red spider mite is controlled by a predatory mite, *Phytoseiulus persimilis*. These and other biological controls can be ordered through some garden centres or from mail order suppliers.

Native bees are worth mentioning here, even though they are not needed to keep down pests or diseases. Their role is in pollination: a high population of native bees will improve the quality and quantity of your crops, simply because they are fantastic pollinators. Problems with pollination are frustrating for gardeners, as unpollinated fruit will often look as if it has set and is going to develop into delicious fruit, only to drop off the tree at a later date. You cannot buy the creatures themselves, but you can buy homes that they will find and colonize. Different-sized homes are available for each type of bee. Red mason bees fly and feed early in the year from March to July, and so are particularly useful for pollinating tree fruit such as apples, pears and plums, and soft fruit such as strawberries, which flower at these times. Blue mason bees fly and feed from May to September, and so are more useful for those vegetables that require pollination for a good crop, such as beans and marrows. The homes are bundles of small hollow tubes placed together, into which the bees crawl and lay their eggs before sealing them off. In autumn, you should remove the home from the allotment and store it in a cool, frost-free place until the following spring, when it can be brought out again and re-hung, preferably near the crop you are hoping to pollinate. Bumblebees are good all-round pollinators, and homes are also available for these.

Hedgehogs and slow worms are also useful creatures to have about, mainly because of their love of slugs. You can buy smart hedgehog homes, in which hedgehogs can hibernate over winter, or you can create a dry and cosy home out of logs. Logs also provide a habitat for slow worms and many other creatures. If you have no access to logs, one of the best slow worm shelters is a piece of corrugated iron, left on the ground.

SPRAYING

There are some problems that can only be controlled by spraying. Potato and tomato blight are particularly tricky to control, and if you live in an area in which it is frequently a problem, it may be worth considering a pre-emptive strike. Copper oxychloride and Bordeaux mixture can be used as a preventative spray, applied before there is any sign of attack. These fungicides are considered suitable for use in organic systems and can also be used to treat other fungal problems. Sulphur dust is also considered suitable for organic gardeners and can be used to control powdery mildew. Take care to follow instructions on timing, application rates and the length of time between spraying and harvesting when using any garden sprays. Even if sprays are called organic, that does not mean they are good to eat.

Sometimes you can use plants themselves to solve problems. Onion leaves can be used in the fight against white rot, a nasty fungal disease of alliums. White rot spores, once they have infected a plant, will lie in the ground for years until another allium plant is planted there, and then leap into action. It can take at least ten years of not growing alliums in that area for the spores to die out. However, if you chop up some onion leaves and dig them into the soil of the affected area, the spores will migrate on to them and go to work. The leaves, not being attached to a living plant, soon die, and the spores die with them.

SOME OPTIONAL EXTRAS

While the half-hour ideal is all about getting in and out quickly, taking no prisoners, there is no harm in considering a few luxuries. None of them is essential to the effective management of your plot, but they may make life more pleasant. The inclusion of a sheltered area with seating on your allotment can provide a place for rest and reflection and make it a nice place to spend some time on a summer evening; a shed is definitely worth considering if you want to be more organised. If you have children to look after, you may wonder if you they are compatible with allotment life; in this chapter you will find a few ideas to encourage them to spend more time with you in the fresh air.

SEATING AND SHELTER

If you are a full-time working, child-rearing or appointment-attending half-hour allotmenteer, you will not have time to sit down on your plot. Your half hour will be efficiently divided into ten-minute portions, with no time in between for rest and recuperation. Once your half hour is up you will be gone, leaving nothing but a trail of decapitated weeds and neatly trimmed edges in your wake. If you are not on quite such a strict timetable, however, you might have time to fit in a few minutes of rest between each ten-minute bout, or a little sunbathe once you've finished. For those who get easily worn out, or who suffer from aches and pains, some seating and a little shelter can be a godsend. If

you are a beginner and a little unsure of local conditions or unsteady on your gardening knowledge, it is handy to have a place to sit your neighbour down and give them a cup of tea from your flask and a biscuit, while you lightly grill them for all their hard-earned gardening knowledge.

Seating may be nothing more elaborate than a lump of wood or the step of your shed, but you could go further and create a bench from scraps you find lying around the site, or even buy one especially for the purpose. A couple of neat stacks of bricks and a plank of wood would be perfect. If you are not the DIY type, a fold-out camping chair makes perfect allotment seating, as it is light and easy to move about, but folds up flat for shed storage.

Creating shade and shelter may seem like a lot of effort, but on a baking hot summer's day or during a fit of spring showers, being able to duck under cover can make the difference between finishing what you've started and abandoning all for home and a dry set of socks. You may have a tree on your plot that is large enough to give you cover, and if it is of a suitable shape you could even suspend a tarpaulin between the branches to create a dry seating area. Pieces of wood hammered together to create a small porch, with a piece of roll-out bamboo screen tacked to the top, castaway-style, look great. A piece of clear plastic secured over the top would make it waterproof. You can also use a shelter as a practical extension of your allotment. A rough framework of well-secured bamboo canes can be used to support sweet peas, peas or beans, which will create their own shade just when it is most needed. Builder's pallets are particularly useful for this kind of thing. They could be stacked end on end and fastened together to make walls, or simply be laid on the floor of your shelter to create a mud-free island. Old patio slabs or even just planks of wood could be put to work as flooring. Always check allotment regulations before building or assembling any kind of permanent structure.

As well as all the practical reasons for creating seating and shelter, there are good psychological ones too. The more structures and permanent features you can put into place on your allotment, the more manageable it becomes. Once your feature is in place, there is less space available to be taken over by weeds, and when everything is mud and dry grass in the depths of winter, you at least have something to prevent that blasted heath look. The lengths you go to with your seating and shelter will really depend on allotment regulations and how much time you plan to spend on your allotment, and that will probably depend on whether you have access to a garden or other outdoor space. If it is to be your substitute garden, it is definitely worth putting in a little effort to make your rest times more comfortable. Site seats and shelters somewhere that will receive sun when you want it, and somewhere near your shed, but away from your compost bins.

AN ALLOTMENT FOR CHILDREN

There are many good reasons for making allotments into places where children – if you have them – can spend time. The first is purely practical. You need to put time in if you are to look after your plot properly, and if you have children to look after as well, you need to find something for them to do while you are on the allotment. If they love visiting it too they will be happy to tag along and will be much less likely to make a fuss about wanting to go home to watch telly just ten minutes after you have arrived. You will also avoid getting into complex childcare arrangements every time you want to pop up to the plot for half an hour. Very young children, however much they like being on the allotment, may require more supervision than you can properly give them while working on your plot. It pays to be realistic from the outset.

Beyond such practicalities, there are perhaps more worthy reasons. There can be few better all-round educational activities than gardening. Many children grow up having no idea where a pea or a tomato actually comes from, and this gap in knowledge prevents them appreciating the difference between good, fresh food and junk. Creating a sense of wonder at growing and harvesting food at an early age will help to set them up for a lifetime of healthy eating. If they have grown a crop themselves, nurturing it from seed to harvest, they are much more likely to want to at least try eating it than if it is all ready prepared for them and plonked on a plate.

Many parents use small pets such as hamsters or goldfish to teach their children about responsibility and nurturing, but this can be a bit of a gamble. Small children, or those with particularly short attention spans, can quickly get bored, and the choice to the parent quickly becomes whether to take on the pet care for themselves or leave the poor little thing to suffer. Usually, the parent steps in and the child only learns that its mum will bail it out if it can't be bothered to do something. Gardening, on the other hand, introduces children to a gentle discipline without the heavy responsibility of the fate of a small mammal resting in their hands. Most parents (militant vegans excepted) will be able to cope with a couple of tomato plants dying, whereas they would feel the need to intervene with a starved and desperate gerbil. The child with plants to care for learns cause and effect: care for it and it lives; neglect it and it dies. Not a bad lesson to take on early in life.

On a more academic note, there are many opportunities for teaching a bit of basic science up the allotment. Pollination, germination, changing seasons, ripening fruits: the curious child will see all these happening around them and will want to know why and how. Most of us, no matter how non-academic our backgrounds, are up to explaining the basics, and it might even make certain conversations a little less painful if they already understand what that bee is doing to that apple blossom.

One final reason is for the memories. Anyone who spent any amount of time in a garden in their childhood will remember them as magical places of play and discovery. A child will look back on quality time spent with you on your allotment with great pleasure and nostalgia for the rest of their lives, no matter how hard it was in reality to actually get them up there.

So how do you get kids involved? Children are territorial creatures and will relish the opportunity of caring for their own patch of ground, so give them their own area to look after. Particularly if they share a room with a sibling, or if they have no other access to a garden, a space of their own will be a matter of great pride and enjoyment; a place where they can really express themselves without their little brother or big sister cramping their style. If you have more than one child, don't be mean and make them share but give them an area each, even if that means giving them less space.

In fact, a child's plot needs to be fairly small in order to be manageable. A square 2m (6ft) by 1.2m (4ft), or a strip 2.5m (8ft) by 0.6m (2ft), should be more than enough for starters. Giving them an unworkable burden would be counter-productive. You might consider delineating their area by making it into a raised bed. This would involve digging the area over and removing all traces of weeds, before lining the edges of the bed with planks of wood or similar, and then

Allotmenteering can be fun, educational and rewarding for children, as well as providing life-long memories

filling in with topsoil, garden compost, manure and possibly grit and sand, if the soil is heavy. The idea is that all the really tough work that might put them off is done for them before they start, in order set them off on an optimistic foot. It may seem expensive to buy in a load of topsoil but it will be a worthwhile investment. You want to make it incredibly easy for them to succeed, at least at first, and by the time you are ready for them to get going, the soil should be the best you have on the plot.

Just as plots should be small and manageable, so should tools. Don't expect a child to struggle on with a set of normal-sized tools. They will find them heavy and unwieldy and there is every possibility that they might hurt themselves with them. The long handles of rakes and spades are also positively hazardous to other children near by (as well as adults, plants and shed windows). Although it may seem excessive, a set of sturdy, colourful, child-sized tools will make children far more likely to stick to their tasks.

What they grow will depend to a certain extent on what they eat. If they have favourite vegetables it is definitely worth including them, but there are also some plants that are sure-fire winners with most kids. Radishes are great, simply because they germinate and grow so fast, but unfortunately they are a little too peppery for most children's tastes. Carrots are probably the next best things in terms of the speed with which they develop into edible plants, and their sweet taste, especially when young, makes them a favourite. Encourage your child to sow them close together and then to thin them as they grow, eating the sweet, tender thinnings immediately. Tomatoes are good, especially the small, sweet, cherry varieties such as 'Sweet 100s' that they can pop into their mouths the moment they are ripe, although they will take a little more patience and dedication than carrots. New potatoes may not seem an obvious choice, but in fact children love the process of digging them up and discovering the buried treasure under the ground. You can then continue their food education by taking the potatoes home to boil, blob with butter and eat that night. Big and bold plants will always hold a special place in the hearts of children, most of whom love to win above all else. Giant pumpkin and sunflower competitions will spur them on to take the best possible care of their charges, even if organized just between family and friends, but particularly if they culminate in a public event where they can really show off, such as an allotment show.

Showing where potatoes come from is a fun part of harvesting with children on an allotment

For outsized pumpkins give them seeds of 'Atlantic Giant' and for the tallest possible sunflowers go for 'Giant Single'.

There are other ways of harnessing children's competitive instincts at the allotment. I recently saw an allotment neighbour with a couch-grass infested area to clear; this patch was cleared within ten minutes by offering the three children in her charge 'a penny a root'. Particularly big roots qualified for 2p or even 3p (to discourage sly chopping up of big ones) and an extra 20p was offered to the child who gathered the most. The kids had soon gathered a mound of roots each. She had kept them occupied while she finished her work, and had a weed-free patch of land for an outlay of little over £1, while they went away chuffed that they had made a bit of sweet money. The key to the success of this kind of bribery and corruption is not to push your luck. Allotting a fairly short amount of time (say ten minutes) and restricting the area to be cleared (perhaps a square metre/yard or two each) will help them believe that it is a real competition and not a dastardly parental trick to get them to do the backbreaking work for peanuts. Plan ahead and have the money to hand to help suspend any suspicions that they are being taken for a ride.

Create areas of your plot where children can just hang out and play safely. Allotments are not places where you want kids to run wild. There are bamboo canes sticking out of the ground and bits of glass and rusting metal hanging around under long grass that they could hurt

themselves on. Not all allotment gardeners are child friendly either, and you may end up getting complaints if your little darlings are too excitable and on too loose a rein. If you have grassed over part of your plot while you work on making a smaller area usable, this spare area can make a perfect child-friendly spot. Create fun features such as a willow stem den. Just push pieces of willow into the ground and bend them over and tie them together to create corridors or play houses. Once pushed into the ground the stems take root, and the entire structure is soon covered in fresh, green leaves, providing privacy for young adventurers. Slides, covered sandpits, climbing frames and swings would be good additions to this sort of area, as would self-contained games such as swingball, but remember to check for allotment restrictions before you start. Normal ball games should certainly be discouraged as they can wreak havoc on sheds, plants, ripe produce and neighbourly relations.

STRUCTURING CHILDREN'S TIME

You may find that once children have caught the bug, they do not need this sort of distraction or too much supervision and are happy to work away under their own steam. Children have short attention spans, however, and it can be worth creating a gardening timetable that panders to this. You can easily adapt the half-hour system to suit them. Perhaps create a quarter-hour system. Children will get bored of any dull jobs within a few minutes, but they should learn that weeding and digging are essential parts of gardening. Bearing this in mind, break up their quarter hour into three five-minute slots, each five minutes to be spent on a different job. So one day's work might include five minutes each of watering, weeding and preparing a bed for seed sowing. The next day might be earthing up potatoes, watering and sowing seeds. Just as with your own time, the pattern of jobs will change with the seasons. If you can make each job well defined in terms of the time allotted, it will prevent your child from seeing gardening as an endless battle with no end in sight, and instead seeing it as a series of small, achievable tasks. A practical way to enforce this is to buy each child a simple wind-up egg timer, which they or you can set as they start each job to go off after five minutes. This way they can easily measure the time for themselves. Once they have finished their fifteen minutes' work, they can have free time to play in their play area, or to help you out.

A CUT FLOWER GARDEN

Dedicating an area to cut flowers goes a little beyond the strict half-hour remit, but a cut flower garden can be a wonderful addition to an allotment. It can be seen as a logical extension of the idea of growing 'dinner-party food'. Flowers, too, are at their best when fresh, and expensive to buy; as you pop up to the allotment to dig your fresh new potatoes ten minutes before your guests arrive, you can pick a vaseful of sweet peas to put on the table.

The main reason to grow flowers at the allotment is for cutting, although you may well enjoy the more colourful look they bring to the plot as well. If you are keen on having cut flowers in the house, you will have a greater and far more imaginative range of flowers to choose from if you grow your own. It is far better to grow flowers for cutting on the allotment, rather than at home in the garden. For one thing you can grow them in bulk so that you can get a really generous bunch every time, without having to put your entire garden over to tulips or daffodils for instance. Secondly, your garden is principally for spending time in and enjoying, while the allotment's main purpose is production. With flowers growing in a garden you will be torn between wanting the garden to look good and wanting to pick flowers for the house; on the allotment there is no such dilemma, as the flowers are there to be picked.

Many of the flowers traditionally grown on allotments make wonderful cut flowers. The old favourites include sweet peas (*Lathyrus odoratus* cultivars), wallflowers (*Erysimum*), gladioli, dahlias, spray chrysanthemums, daffodils (*Narcissus*) and irises. They have become associated with allotments as they are all good competition flowers that would have been primped and cosseted for the allotment or village show. All benefit from growing in the big, light, open areas that are more often found on allotments than in gardens and they love the intensive care and lack of competition. Bulbs, corms and perennial plants are particularly useful for the gardener with limited time, as they come up year after year and so need minimum attention to get them started. Among the perennials you could include roses, peonies and alchemilla, and good bulbs include daffodils (*Narcissus*), tulips, hyacinths, lilies and ornamental onions (*Allium*). All make great cut flowers.

Along with sweet peas, which need to be sown from seed each year, there are a number of other annuals that are fairly straightforward to get going. Sweet peas really need starting off early in pots under cover. Ideally they are sown in autumn to give them plenty of time to get going so that the flowers arrive good and early the following summer, but you can buy plants in spring that have been started off for you. The more sweet pea flowers you pick, the more the plants will produce. This makes them worth a little extra trouble. Other annuals can be direct sown in autumn or spring. Good ones to consider for autumn or early spring sowing are cornflowers (*Centaurea cyanus*), poppies (*Papaver*), marigolds (*Calendula*), honesty (*Lunaria annua*) and scabious.

Organize your cut flowers so that you have perennials and bulbs in one area, where they will be disturbed relatively rarely, and then leave space for your annuals in another area. Bulbs and perennials are best planted in rows, in order to fit as many in as possible, unless you are trying to create a garden feel to the cut-flower bed.

Bear in mind that some annuals, such as sweet peas, will need structures to climb up. These can be made from bamboo sticks tied together with string, or from frames of wood with pea netting strung between them. The important thing is to position them on the northernmost edge of your flower bed, so that the climbing annuals do not cast shade over the other flowers as they clamber up their structure.

When sowing annuals direct into the ground, prepare the ground well and rake it to a fine tilth. It is better to create a series of small lines into which to sow the seed, rather than just scattering it over the prepared area. Although this looks regimented at first, it will help you to distinguish the flower seeds from weed seeds as they emerge from the soil (probably at about the same time). As the flower seedlings grow you will find that they are too close to each other and you should thin them out in order to give each plant the space it needs to reach maturity and flower. Once you start to thin the rows out, they will lose their uniform look. Remember that although some plants, such as tulips, will only produce one flush of flowers per year, others like sweet peas will keep on producing new flowers as long as you keep picking them, so do this regularly. It won't really be that much of a chore.

AN EASY CUT FLOWER GARDEN
Early autumn is a good time to start a new cut flower area, as it gives you time to put spring bulbs into place. Once you have cleared an area

for growing cut flowers, dig it over well. You can leave most of the area fairly rough, to be worked on by the frosts over winter, but prepare one area well for your spring-flowering bulbs. Tulips and daffodils are good ones to start with. Plant out daffodils by the end of September and tulips by November. Plant at least twenty bulbs of each, in rows, planting them at least three times the depth of the bulb.

In spring you can sow a few annuals. First thoroughly dig over the roughly worked ground until the soil is fine and crumbly. Then mark out little rows several inches apart and water the bottom of these seed drills before sprinkling in seeds of easy annuals such as Shirley poppies (*Papaver rhoeas* Shirley Group cultivars), marigolds (*Calendula*), cornflowers (*Centaurea cyanus*) and honesty (*Lunaria annua*). As these grow, thin them out to their final spacings, which will be given on the seed packet.

Buy pots of sweet pea seedlings from a garden centre in spring, separate them and plant them out next to a sturdy frame of bamboo canes. You will need to tie them in regularly.

Spring is also the time to plant summer bulbs, corms and tubers, such as lilies, dahlias and gladioli. Plant these near the tulips and daffodils, because all these plants can stay in the ground for several years.

A WILDLIFE GARDEN

If you are creating an organic allotment, that is a good reason for having an area that is left a little rough and ready, and in which wildlife can thrive. However, there is always loads of wildlife on all allotments, whether you actively encourage it or not – wildlife is attracted to green spaces – and there are several drawbacks to giving over a whole area to wildlife that you should keep in mind. The first is that they are messy. This is an important consideration if you are trying to keep your plot going with the minimum of time and fuss. Grass and weeds left to grow turn to seed, which can spread all over your own plot and your neighbours'. Slugs and snails can hide in long grass and emerge at night to eat vulnerable seedlings. The fact that wildlife areas usually don't look great will seem to real nature lovers to be a side issue, but it can make life harder if you are trying to keep on top of a plot and you have to get used to sly comments from your neighbours. If your allotment committee is not organically minded, a wildlife area could easily be construed as a neglected area, and this could get you a warning or a threat of eviction. It may be simpler and less time consuming just to put in a few wildlife friendly features, rather than giving over a whole area to wildlife. These could include a small pond, for frogs, and a couple of insect houses. If you do decide to create a wildlife garden on your plot, mow around the perimeter of it regularly and surround it with an edging of sharp gravel. This will make it look smarter and 'deliberate', and it should also help contain the slugs and snails.

A SHED

Sheds are not, strictly speaking, an optional luxury; most people would agree that they can be pretty essential to the efficient running and organisation of an allotment. The way you organize them, however, and the things that you keep in them, can make all the difference. A shed that you just chuck your tools in at the end of a session is fine. It is serving its basic purpose well, but it could certainly do better. Purely in terms of time management, a well-stocked and well-organized shed makes sense. If you have to take everything you might need with you every time you go, you can use up your entire spare half hour just in preparation. A shed will reduce the amount of time it takes you to get out of the house and up to the allotment.

When you first get started, think about shed security. Allotments are empty and lonely places at night, and as such are irresistible to thieves and vandals. Most theft on allotments is opportunistic. It is caused by bored kids with nothing better to do and only rarely will there be a properly organized attempt on your tools. Thieves are after things with good resale value, such as new, shiny, high-quality tools and machinery, so if you have anything fitting this description, don't keep it there. Carry any posh bits of kit home with you at the end of a session. Buy a set of old, cheap and battered-looking spades and rakes from a car boot sale and leave those in the shed. If you really must have good ones, and can't carry them back and forth for some reason, at least get them a bit mucky by smearing mud on the shiny bits and on the handles.

You can go one of two ways when it comes to securing the shed. The obvious way is to make sure that the door of your shed fits securely, with good, solid hinges and fixings, and to lock it up with a good, chunky padlock. However, a padlock can act as a bit of a magnet for unwanted attention, making it look as if you have something worth protecting, and many allotment shed doors are not solid enough to withstand said attention for long. A determined allotment thief has all the time in the world and knows he is unlikely to be disturbed in the middle of the night. The alternative may sound a little scary, but it seems to work just as well. It is to not lock your shed at all. Making the shed look as if it is not worth breaking into is at least as good a deterrent as making it look as if it will be hard to break into. For that really ramshackle look, prop the door closed with a couple of bits of wood.

When setting up your shed, consider alternatives to glass windows, as these are particularly attractive to vandals. Put in a piece of thick translucent plastic instead, or just cover the window hole over with a wooden board. If you inherit a shed, spend a little time smartening up the roof to make it weatherproof, as this protects both shed contents and structure from damp. Your allotment society may even supply new roofing felt. Once this is in place, install gutters and a rain barrel, which not only prevent pools of water from forming around the shed after a

heavy downpour but also provide a handy store of water on your plot, preventing the need for you to collect water every time you need it. An extension to the downpipe that can be swung between a series of barrels will allow you to collect water all winter long, even after your first barrel is full.

Some strange allotment societies have rules against erecting sheds. This always seems a real shame, and not only for practical reasons.

Sheds bring so much character – a shedless site can look quite barren and bleak. It also leaves you with a problem regarding tool storage. Often there is a height restriction that effectively excludes sheds, and you can get around this by investing in a long box with a lid that you can cover in roofing felt, to keep it waterproof. Buy one long enough to fit your tools, as well as other bits and pieces. These

also double as seats. As a temporary measure, wrapping your tools in a piece of old carpet keeps them dry and hides them from potential burglars while making your plot look like it contains nothing worth stealing.

In addition to the basic tools that you will keep in your shed, you might also consider including any of the following as permanent residents: a garden line to help you plant or sow in straight lines; plastic bags for harvesting; secateurs; a bucket for collecting weed roots; a pair of old shoes; an old coat; an old sun hat; sun cream; a folding camping chair; a pen and some labels; a hammer, screwdriver, screws and tin of nails for running shed repairs; a plank of wood for standing on and working off; and a tape measure.

Sheds are the heart of any allotment site, providing storage for tools, shelter from the elements and lots of character

10

WHAT NEXT?

This book has, I hope, given you the tools you need to create an allotment that you can manage in tandem with a busy life, rather than one that you have to devote half your life to. If you follow its advice, you should have an allotment that produces the best-tasting crops in the right quantities to supply your and your family's needs, without huge gluts or famines. You should have a supply of seasonal fresh vegetables all year round, all for just half an hour's work a day.

For many allotmenteers this will be enough. The challenge of maintaining an allotment doesn't go away once you have managed to put a system into place. An allotment needs constant attention, even just to keep it at a standstill. If you are working full time, have a busy home life or just don't want to spend very much time gardening, the half-hour system should keep you very happy indeed.

But some people really get the bug and start wanting to develop their allotmenting skills. This final chapter is designed to give you ideas on where to go next, if you feel you have the energy and the time to do more. There are all sorts of things you could put your energy into, but I want to recommend some things that keep you within the basic tenet of the half-hour system: they should either increase the quality of the crops you produce or increase the ease with which you can produce them. Don't put your extra energy into cranking up the quantities; few people are really happy when they produce so many potatoes and onions that they could set up a soup kitchen to feed all their neighbours.

STORAGE

Storage has hardly been touched upon in this book, and with good reason. You should always aim to harvest fresh and eat immediately. This is the way to enjoy your crops when they are at their best. There is something special about eating crops in season. Strawberries in February are a treat, but fresh off the plant at the height of summer they taste like what you ought to be eating.

However, there will be times when you do have more of a certain crop than you can eat immediately. This is particularly the case with fruit trees and bushes, the fruit of which has a tendency to all ripen at around the same time. Try to avoid freezing as far as possible. Unless you have a large chest freezer or two, you will soon run out of space you need for other purposes such as ice cream. The process is generally detrimental to the quality of the produce, which takes on a mushy consistency no matter how fresh and crisp it started off.

If you must freeze, do so as soon as possible after harvesting. First, wash the fruits or vegetables thoroughly and discard any that are not at their best, and trim and cut into serving-sized pieces, as necessary. Vegetables will need to be blanched or briefly steamed and then cooled quickly in icy water before freezing. This step inactivates enzymes that will damage flavour nutrients and texture during freezer storage. After preparation, spread the fruit or vegetables out on a tray covered in baking parchment so that they are not touching, and put the whole lot in the freezer. Once they have frozen, you can bundle them all into a freezer bag or box and pop them back into the freezer. This means that they will not all be stuck together in a big lump when you come to use them, and can be used in small quantities if necessary. They also retain at least some of their original shape, rather than becoming an amorphous blob.

A far more interesting alternative is bottling. When you bottle fruit you have to combine them with syrup or fruit juice, and this process alone can make the crop into a higher-quality product. Some fruits, including tomatoes, can simply be packed into the jars without the need for any solution surrounding them. Remove the skins first, by plunging the fruits into boiling water for a minute and then directly into cold water. The skins should slip off easily. You can also make your crops into ready-to-use sauces such as fruit pie fillings or pasta sauce and bottle those. You will need to buy some special bottling jars and lids (you may find them sold as canning jars: this is the terminology from America, where the practice is far more common).

Sterlize jars, bottles and lids in boiling water and then air-dry before filling with the prepared fruit or sauce. Fruit should be covered in a solution. To make a syrup, boil two parts sugar and eight parts water together until the sugar is dissolved. Pour this or fruit juice over the fruit. Replace the lids and then replace the jars into a large saucepan of water. They should be kept off the base of the saucepan using a wire rack, so that they do not get too hot and crack. Boil for about thirty minutes before removing (you can buy special tongs for this purpose) and leave to cool overnight. You will know that the jars are sealed if the lids have a slight depression and do not move when touched. This is called heat processing and creates a sterile, vacuum-sealed environment inside the container. Make sure that you label everything well, store somewhere dark and cool and use within the year; discard any preserves that have deteriorated or with damaged or swollen seals. If a vacuum seal does not seal after heat processing, refrigerate the product and use within one week.

Of course you can also make jams, chutneys and pickles as a way of using up excess produce and turning your crops into a high-quality product that is easy to store.

Another interesting way of storing excess crops is to dry them. In hot countries with a predictable climate this is done out of doors in the sun. Sun-dried tomatoes and peppers have almost all the moisture evaporated out of them, which intensifies the flavours, and they can be stored for long periods. In Britain we do not often have the luxury of long runs of good weather, but there are other ways of drying foods. If you have a warm conservatory or a particularly warm area of your house, you can just hang bunches of your

Some ways of storing excess crops, such as oven drying or pickling sweet peppers, can actually improve their quality

GROWING UNUSUAL CULTIVARS

Another way in which you might want to branch out on your allotment is in trying out some unusual cultivars. One of the methods this book has suggested to make your life easier is to use the services of plug plant nurseries to buy in small seedlings of certain vegetable plants, where this proves simpler than direct sowing. However, the number and variety of cultivars that are available in the form of plug plants is very limited, and you may find that after a few years you long to experiment with some new, unusual or heritage cultivars. This is always a good idea, as many of the heritage cultivars – old varieties that have disappeared from seed catalogues in favour of different or more fashionable cultivars – have a reputation for doing well under certain difficult circumstances, perhaps similar to your own, and they are often renowned for having a particularly good taste. The newer cultivars may have been bred for resistance to particular diseases or pests that are prevalent on your plot. Start to look out for different catalogues, and talk to fellow allotment holders about the sources of their seeds. Look in the back of gardening magazines, or on the internet, for nurseries that sell unusual ranges of seed, and send off for their catalogues to see if there is anything that appeals to you. Smaller nurseries are often run by real enthusiasts, and you will find it hard to resist their descriptions. Seeds of heritage cultivars may not be available to buy, because of

chosen produce up to dry naturally. This is especially effective if you have an aga or a heater that gives out constant heat. You can also prepare fruit and vegetables on baking trays by slicing them and removing any seeds or leaving as they are, before placing them in an oven on its lowest heat overnight, and with the door propped open to let out the evaporating moisture. The larger the pieces, the longer they will take to dry. If all this sounds like too much fuss, though, you can buy an Italian-style drying machine, which comprises a number of racks on which to place your prepared vegetables. The machine removes excess moisture and you are left with a 'sun-dried' product that can be stored in sterilized jars, either dry or topped up with oil. Drying is suitable for herbs, tomatoes, peppers and chillies, as well as for fruits such as apricots, prunes and apples, and you can experiment with all sorts of crops to see how well they dry.

European legislation that requires all seed for sale to be included on a national or EC list, but they can be sourced through special libraries, such as the HDRA Heritage Seed Library (www.hdra.org.uk/hsl/).

If you decide you want to try experimenting with some of these new and different cultivars, you will have to start sowing your own, rather than buying seedlings in. There is an easy and a difficult way of doing this. The usual way is to start off by sowing your seeds into seed trays, and leaving them to germinate on your windowsill. Once they germinate, you prick them out. This means lifting the individual seedlings by their leaves out of the soil and quickly transferring them into a small pot or module of soil. You then place them back on the windowsill while they grow a bit larger. As the weather starts to warm up in spring, you might start moving them outside during the day to harden them off, but you have to bring them in at night in case of late frosts. You tread a fine line between putting them outside enough to give them plenty of light, and so avoid making them drawn-up and leggy, and leaving them out during weather that is too cold for them. It is hard to get exactly right, and this is why it is such a good idea to get someone else to do this work for you when you first start out.

No matter how experienced you become, sowing your own seeds will always be a skilled job that runs the risk of your suffering losses, growing sub-standard seedlings or, almost as annoyingly, growing far too many seedlings for your needs. But there is a slightly simpler way of going about things. First, forget the whole pricking-out business and sow single seeds straight into your final container, be that pot or module. The drawback to this is that not all will germinate, and so you will have some waste of compost or pots for those that do not. Weigh this small amount of waste up against the palaver of the whole pricking-out business, though, and you will see that it is worth a few empty modules or pots. Simply discard the soil from the pots of ungerminated seed, and the pots can be used again.

Trays of different-sized modules can be bought at garden centres, and these are particularly useful as they hold only a small amount of soil, and so there is less chance of a small seedling getting waterlogged than there would be in a pot. However, they will only really be suitable for small seedlings, and certainly not for larger ones such as courgettes or tomatoes, which must go straight into a pot. Some seeds will seem so small that you may find it impossible to sow one per module. This is not a problem: you can sow a few to a pot and then pull out the weaker seedlings at a later date. Again, this can seem wasteful, but remember that every seed packet is likely to contain enough potential vegetables to serve several families, and so a few lost plants at this stage is not the end of the world. Use the table in chapter 4 to see how many plants you really need. Sow a few more than this to allow for losses, but don't be tempted to sow the whole packet simply because they are there. If they are really bothering you, give them away to a neighbouring plot holder.

If you have a greenhouse or polytunnel (see page 151), this is the ideal place to sow these seeds, to keep them out of the house. Either will be flooded with light and stay almost frost free from mid-spring onwards. But most people, particularly those who are new to gardening or short on space at home, will not have one. Instead of hopelessly lusting after one, invest in a temporary plastic greenhouse.

These structures are usually made of a metal, foldable frame around which is hung a clear plastic covering. This can be zipped up at night to keep the cold out, or unzipped for easy access or to allow ventilation on warmer days. They provide enough protection and let in enough light for your seedlings to thrive, but are usually extremely compact. The most common design is tall and slender; it comprises a number of shelves stacked on top of each other, yet is narrow and so fits into even the smallest back garden. The real beauty of these temporary structures is that they can be folded up and put away in the loft or the shed as soon as they are no longer in use, once you've put the plants out on to the allotment. A drawback is that they are not as insulated as greenhouses and so plants inside them are more vulnerable to frost. You may have to cover them with a blanket or a layer of bubble wrap on particularly cold spring nights, in which case it is essential to remember to remove the extra covering in the morning – otherwise the plants will not receive enough

light. It is worth noting that plants will grow more slowly in a temporary greenhouse than they would indoors or in a permanent greenhouse, because they are not in such warm conditions. However, this can be a bonus, as they will not get so drawn up, and they will be hardier and tougher when the time comes for them to go out on to the allotment, and so better able to resist any late frosts or adverse conditions.

A compact alternative to temporary greenhouses is a cold frame. These low boxes with glass lids can be utilized in the same way. They are a more permanent, though, as they are often made from wood and glass and are therefore heavy and cumbersome to move out of the way after you have planted out your seedlings.

With all seedlings that you grow yourself, there will need to be a period of hardening off to prevent them from getting too much of a shock when they are first planted out. Start off by opening the zips of the greenhouse during warm days, always closing them again at night. Move on to fully opening up the greenhouse in the day and closing it at night, and eventually, near planting out time, and when you know that the danger of frost has passed, leave it open all the time. The last frost date for your area will be anywhere between March and June, depending on a number of factors, including how built up your area is, and its latitude, altitude and proximity to the sea. If you are not sure of the likely last frost date for your area, remember to check the local weather forecasts regularly, and to close up the greenhouse if frost threatens.

Even if you can make a rough guess, every year will be different, and there is always a danger of a sneaky, late frost. It is better to be safe than to lose a whole load of seedlings in one night.

POLYTUNNELS

After a couple of years on your allotment, you are quite likely to start hankering after a polytunnel. I say polytunnel, rather than greenhouse, with good reason. Greenhouses are not really suitable for the allotment. They are usually expensive, they are magnets for vandals, and panes of glass are easily broken. You may find yourself regularly having to replace glass – an unpleasant and expensive job. Greenhouses look nice in a garden, but on an allotment such considerations are less important. A polytunnel is cheaper and will do the job just as well.

There are a couple of reasons for considering a polytunnel on an allotment: they extend the seasons in which you can grow certain crops, and they improve the quality of the crops that you are already producing. At the beginning of the year you will be able to plant out your more tender vegetables such as melons, courgettes, peppers and aubergines weeks before you could outside, and without the danger of them being affected by frost. This will mean that they will start cropping earlier in the year. You can use a polytunnel as a space for bringing on seedlings, should you decide that you want to, and so avoid the need to erect even a temporary home greenhouse. In this sense

polytunnels can be particularly useful for those who have no garden at home, or just a small courtyard. At the end of the summer, you can use a polytunnel to ripen fruits that need a long season: you will end up with far fewer green tomatoes to dispose of at the end of the summer if you grow tomatoes under a polytunnel. Over winter, a polytunnel provides a place that is sufficiently sheltered for many things to be able to keep growing more strongly than they would out of doors, allowing you to continue to crop young, tender lettuce leaves and carrots throughout the coldest months, rather than relying on the tough old things that have been out in the worst of the weather.

A final reason for having a polytunnel is that it is handy to have somewhere on your plot that is always warm and dry, and where you have control over the elements. It is a great place for curing vegetables such as pumpkins and garlic, which need a warm, dry spell and good ventilation if they are to store well. A polytunnel also allows you to spend time at the allotment during the wettest weather.

It is true that the majority of these functions – particularly extending the seasons – are also fulfilled by small cloches that you place over rows of plants out of doors. A polytunnel is just a more luxurious, more expensive way of getting the same effect, but as such it may inspire you to try more tender vegetables at trickier times of the year.

A polytunnel comprises a metal frame with a skin of plastic stretched over it. Have a look around your site and see what size tunnels other people have. If you can get a look inside one, all the better. This will give you an idea of whether your idea of what you can grow in a certain-sized polytunnel is realistic. You may have to upgrade. Generally the larger the polytunnel, the better. You will find that you soon fill it up, so buy the largest you can fit into the space available. Before you buy, though, check your site's rules; some have height restrictions that would forbid the erection of a polytunnel, or other restrictions that might affect which size you go for. Be aware, too, that you will need to manage your polytunnel, and having one will add to the list of jobs you have to do regularly. For instance, in winter the doors will be permanently shut, but there will be times in late spring when you may need to open the doors in the morning and return to close them up at night, so as to keep the temperature relatively stable.

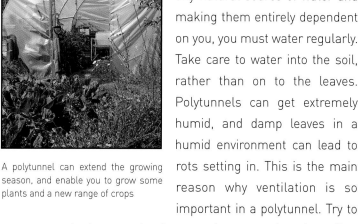

A polytunnel can extend the growing season, and enable you to grow some plants and a new range of crops

It is important that you clear the site well before you erect a polytunnel. Once it is up, it will provide a warm and often humid environment – perfect growing conditions for most plants, including weeds. Treat the soil of the polytunnel area as thoroughly as you would a new piece of ground that you were about to start planting up, if not more so. When setting the polytunnel up, it is a good idea to lay a path up its centre. This could be made from paving stones, gravel, woodchips or even grass. A table at about waist height can be extremely useful in a polytunnel. It can be a propagating bench in spring, or you can use it as extra growing space when you run out. You may also want to use it to raise seedlings up off the ground to keep them away from slugs.

Watering is extremely important in a polytunnel. Since you are cutting plants off from any natural source of water and making them entirely dependent on you, you must water regularly. Take care to water into the soil, rather than on to the leaves. Polytunnels can get extremely humid, and damp leaves in a humid environment can lead to rots setting in. This is the main reason why ventilation is so important in a polytunnel. Try to buy one that has openings at each end, to allow for a complete exchange of air. Ventilation will be most important at the height of summer, when polytunnels can really overheat and cause plants to wilt, but it will be necessary in warm spells during other seasons too.

Although plants can be planted straight into the soil inside a polytunnel, it can be a good idea to use growing bags or large pots of soil instead. This is because the space within a polytunnel is pretty limited, and so you do not have the space to put a real system of rotation into place. If you grow tomatoes in the same spot in the polytunnel year after year, you will get a build-up of tomato pests and diseases in the soil. Pots and growing bags will give you more watering work but this will be worth it in the long run.

ALLOTMENT FAIR

The time will come when you feel so confident of the crops you are producing that you are ready to try your luck at the local allotment fair or flower show. Times have changed on allotments, and growing the longest leek or the largest pumpkin is no longer considered the pinnacle of success. You are more likely to measure your success by how often you have fresh, delicious, tender vegetables on your dinner plate, rather than by their size, but there is still a place for you at the fair. At the least it is an opportunity to meet fellow allotmenteers and to have a bit of fun; it can also be a chance to show off your achievements.

It is true that in some places you will still find a group of old boys competing fiercely to produce the straightest runner bean, but on most sites you will be surprised at how well your produce measures up, and it is always worth having a go. You do not need to have been paying your chosen vegetable constant attention or feeding it with a specially formulated fertilizer. The most important criterion for the judging of vegetables in allotment shows is actually not size at all but uniformity. If it is the height of summer and your produce is ripening daily, you should have plenty to choose from. Look for vegetables with good shiny skin, and that are similar in size and shape. Clean them well and trim them, and then present them neatly arranged on a plate.

Your secret weapon, however, will be flavour. In many allotment shows the judges will not just look at the produce but taste it too. If you have made it your mission to produce only the tastiest, most tender vegetables for your own table, the judges will appreciate this, especially if they compare them with larger but tougher or more watery offerings. You will have an extra advantage if you have started to use more unusual or heritage cultivars, as these will provide different flavours from those of your competitors and make your produce stand out.

There will also usually be awards given for products made from allotment produce. If you have made any pickles, dried or bottled fruits or jams, this is the place to get them out and have them judged. Again, presentation is important, and your jars should be tidy and neatly labelled, but it is taste that will win the day.

With a bit of luck you will come away with a clutch of certificates, but at the very least you will have a lot of fun and have a chance to swap tips with your fellow allotmenteers on coping with your specific conditions and the best cultivars. And if you do win a few prizes, it will be confirmation that allotments are all about the eating, and that you are eating the very best.

NEXT PAGE A well-planned, smooth-running allotment will become easier to manage as the years go by, inspiring you to try new things

FURTHER READING

Grow Your Own Vegetables, by Joy Larkcom (Frances Lincoln, 2002)

Organic Gardening, by Lawrence D. Hills (Penguin, 1977)

RHS Pests and Diseases, by Pippa Greenwood and Andrew Halstead (Dorling Kindersley, 2003)

RHS Fruit and Vegetable Gardening, by Michael Pollock (Dorling Kindersley, 2002)

HDRA Encyclopedia of Organic Gardening, editor-in-chief Pauline Pears (Dorling Kindersley, 2005)

The Vegetable and Herb Expert, by D.G. Hessayon (Expert Books, 1997)

The Fruit Expert, by D.G. Hessayon (Expert Books, 1991)

RHS Horticultural Show Handbook (Royal Horticultural Society) This is a useful book if you get serious about showing your fruit and veg at local competitions

RHS AGM Plants (Royal Horticultural Society) This biennial publication is useful for its listing and description of fruit and vegetable varieties recommended by the RHS

RHS membership, either as a gift or for yourself, is certainly a helpful investment. As well as free access to all four RHS gardens, you have access to free gardening advice and the RHS monthly magazine, *The Garden*. This magazine is full of practical advice, ideas and inspiration, and every issue will contain something relevant to the allotment gardener. Tel: 0845 067 0000 for more information.

Also visit the RHS online at www.rhs.org.uk, where you will find a wealth of information.

SOME MAIL ORDER SUPPLIERS

CHILTERN SEEDS
Bortree Stile, Ulverston, Cumbria
LA12 7PB
Tel: 01229 581137
Fax: 01229 584549
www.chilternseeds.co.uk
Suppliers of a very interesting selection of vegetable and herb seeds

DELFLAND NURSERIES LTD
Benwick Road, Doddington, March, Cambridgeshire PE15 0TU
Tel: 01354 740553
Fax: 01354 741200
www.organicplants.co.uk
Suppliers of organic vegetable plants

KEN MUIR

Honeypot Farm, Rectory Road, Weeley Heath,
Clacton-on-Sea, Essex CO16 9BJ

Tel: 0870 7479111

Fax: 01255 831534

www.kenmuir.co.uk

Fruit growers and distributors of certified stock

MARSHALLS SEEDS

Alconbury Hill, Huntingdon, Cambridgeshire
PE28 4HU

Tel: 01480 443390

Fax: 01480 443391

www.marshalls-seeds.co.uk

Suppliers of vegetable plants plus a good
range of fruit trees and plants

THE ORGANIC GARDENING CATALOGUE

Riverdene, Molesey Road, Hersham, Surrey
KT12 4RG

Tel: 0845 130 1304

Fax: 01932 252707

www.organiccatalogue.com

The official mail order catalogue of the HDRA,
the organic association. RHS and HDRA
members get a 10 per cent discount. Heritage
varieties available

THE REAL SEED CATALOGUE

Brithdir Mawr, Newport, Pembrokeshire
SA42 0QJ

Tel: 01239 821107

www.realseeds.co.uk

A particularly good source of unusual
Mediterranean cultivars, all trialled by the
owners for their suitability to cooler climates

SIMPSONS SEEDS

The Walled Garden Nursery, Horningsham,
Wiltshire BA12 7NQ.

Tel: 01985 845004

Suppliers of vegetable seeds and seedlings,
specializing in hard-to-find and less well-
known varieties

SUFFOLK HERBS

Monks Farm, Coggeshall Road, Kelvedon,
Essex CO5 9PG

Tel: 01376 572456

Fax: 01376 571189

www.suffolkherbs.com

Suppliers of organically produced seed

INDEX

A

access 19
alchemilla 139
alliums 110, 121–2, 139
   see also garlic; onions
alyssum 122
ants 124–5
aphids 122, 123, 124–5, 128
apples 41, 42, 50, 125, 148
   'Park Farm Pippin' 50
   'Pinova' 50
   'Red Falstaff' 50
asparagus 41, 50
   'Backlim' 50
   'Gijnlim' 50
   'Jersey Knight' 50
aubergines 51, 95, 100, 151
   'Mohican' 51
   'Purple Prince' 51
   'Red Egg' 51
   'Slicerite' 51
autumn work programme 115

B

beans 24, 51–2, 103, 122
   support 96, 99
   see also broad beans;
      dwarf French beans
beer traps 126
bees 128–9
beetroot 38, 52
   'Boltardy' 52
   'Detroit Globe' 52
biological controls 125–6,
   127–9
birds 123
black plastic mulches 84
blackberries 42
blackcurrants 41, 42, 96
blackfly 122, 126–7
bottling 147, 153
boysenberries 61
brambles 19
brassicas 24, 32, 95, 103
   pests and diseases 120,
   121–2, 123
   see also different types of
      brassica
broad beans 38, 51, 126–7
   'Imperial Green Longpod'
   51
   'Super Aquadulce' 51
broccoli 32, 53
Brussels sprouts 32, 53
   'Braveheart' 121
   'Cavalier' 121
   'Cromwell' 53
   'Noisette' 53
   'Red Delicious' 53

C

cabbage 32, 54–5, 86
cabbage root fly 121–2, 123,
   124
cabbage white butterflies 123
calabrese 53
   'Belstar' 53
   'Hydra' 53
   'Trixie' 53
camomile 122
cardboard mulches 84
carpet mulches 84
carrot fly 121, 123, 124, 127
carrots 55, 100, 151
   sowing 38, 78, 95, 103
   'Early Nantes' 55
   'Flyaway' 121
   'Nanco' 55
   'Paris Market' 55
   'Primo' 55
   'Resistafly' 121
   'Sytan' 55
cauliflower, 'Castlegrant' 56
celeriac, 'Monarch' 56
chard 57
   'Bright Lights' 57
   'White Silver' 57
chemicals *see* fungicides;
   herbicides; pesticides
cherries 42, 125
chicken manure 94
chicory 57
   'Jupiter' 57
   'Palla Rossa' 57
   'Witloof' 57
children 133–8
chilli peppers 148
   'Anaheim' 64
   'Thai Dragon' 64
Chinese cabbage 63
chrysanthemums 138
clay soils 28, 90, 92
cloches 100, 126
   see also cold frames
club root 103, 120
cold frames 150
   see also cloches
companion planting 121–2
compost 25, 100–102
coriander 122
cornflowers 122, 139, 140
costs 14–15, 37
couch grass 25, 85, 137
courgettes 58, 86, 95, 149,
   151
   'Custard White' 58
   'De Nice a Fruit Rond' 58
   'Gold Rush' 58
   'Kojak' 58

crop rotation 24, 102–3, 120,
   152
crops, choosing 32–5, 46
cultivars 46, 121, 148–51
curly kale 32, 59
   'Red Bor' 59
   'Winterbor' 59
cut flowers 138–40

D

daffodils 138, 139, 140
dahlias 138, 140
digging 83, 111
diseases 24, 103, 120–29
drainage 20
drying fruit and vegetables
   147–8
dwarf French beans 34, 38,
   51, 78, 95
   'Delinell' 51
   'Triomph de Farcy
      Stringless' 51

E

edging, wood 27, 28
education 133–4
ericaceous soils 28

F

fairs 153
fallow areas 86–7, 137
fennel 122
fertilizer 93–4
feverfew 122
fleece 24, 99, 123
foxgloves 122
freezing 146–7
French beans *see* dwarf
   French beans
French marigolds 122
frost 20, 99–100, 149, 150–51
fruit cages 123
fruit trees 41–2, 99–100, 123,
   125
fungicides 129

G

garlic 58, 151
   'Roja' 58
   'Solent Wight' 58
   'Thermidrome' 58
garlic chives 121–2
gladioli 138, 140
gluts 47
glyphosate 79
good-value plants 34–5
gooseberries 41, 42, 96
green manures 85–6
green-in-the-snow 63
greenhouses 128, 150, 151

H

half-hour principle 12–15, 87,
   106
half-plots 19, 20–21
hardening off 149, 150
harvesting 107–8
hedgehogs 129
herbicides 78–82
herbs 28, 122, 148
heritage cultivars 148–9, 153
hoeing 116
honesty 139, 140
hyacinths 139

I

inorganic fertilizers 94
irises 138

J

Japanese knotweed 19

K

kale 32, 59

L

lacewings 121, 128
ladybirds 128
lavender 122
leeks 59
   'Apollo' 59
   'Bulgarian Giant' 59
   'Conora' 121
   'Musselburgh' 59
lettuce 34, 60, 95, 122, 151
   sowing 38, 78
   'Avon Crisp' 121
   'Barcelona' 121
   'Little Gem' 121
lilies 139, 140
lime 93
loam 92
loganberries 41, 42, 61

M

mail order 38, 156–7
mangetout 34, 61, 99
   'Oregon Sugar Pod' 61
manure 19, 92, 103
marigolds 139, 140
marjoram 122
melons 62, 95, 100, 151
   'Castella' 62
   'Sweetheart' 62
mint 122
mizuna 63
mowing and edging 26, 86,
   110
mulches 84
mustards 60, 63

N

nasturtiums 122
neighbours 87
nematodes 127, 128
new potatoes 35, 65, 99, 136
  'Accent' 121
  'Anya' 65
  'Epicure' 65
  'Foremost' 121
  'Home Guard' 65
  'Kestrel' 121
  'Swift' 65
nitrogen 94, 103
nursery beds 35, 37

O

onion downy mildew 120
onions 34, 38, 69, 103, 129
organic matter 92–3, 100–102
organic methods
  fertilizers 94
  pest control 120–29
  weeds 78, 82–6
  wildlife 140
oriental leaves 63

P

pak choi 63
parsnips 38, 103
paths 23–4, 25–8, 79
peaches 42
pears 41, 42, 63, 125
  'Comice' 63
  'Concorde' 63
  'William' 63
peas 32, 34, 61, 99, 103
peonies 139
peppers 64, 147, 148, 151
perennial weeds 25, 83, 85,
  86
permanent plants 39–42, 96,
  139
permanent structures 132,
  141–3
pesticides 120
pests 24, 34, 103, 120–29
  slugs and snails 26, 39,
    125–6, 128, 140
pH tests 93
phosphorus 94
picking 107–8
planning
  layout 23–5
  planting 47–8, 108
  upkeep 107–10
plots
  choosing 18–20
  getting started 76–8
  planning layout 23–5
  sharing 23

size 20–21, 32
  upkeep 106–111, 114–16
plug plants 37–8
plums 41, 42, 125
poached egg plants 122
pollination 122, 128–9
polytunnels 151–3
poppies 139, 140
potassium 94
potato blight 129
potatoes 24, 95, 122
  maincrop 34, 78
  resistant cultivars 121
  and weeds 86, 103
  'Cara' 121
  'Lady Balfour' 121
  'Sante' 121
  'Sarpo' 121
  see also new potatoes
powdery mildew 129
pumpkins 86, 136–7, 151

Q

quantities to sow 47

R

rain barrels 141–2
raised beds 27–8, 134, 136
raspberries 41, 42, 66, 95
  support 96
  'Autumn Bliss' 66
  'Joan J' 66
red spider mite 128
redcurrants 41, 42, 67, 96
  'Red Nose' 67
  'Rovada' 67
resistant cultivars 121
rhubarb 41, 67
  'Champagne' 67
  'Stockbridge Arrow' 67
roses 139
rotation 24, 102–3, 120, 152
rotovators 85
runner beans 52, 95
  support 96, 99
  'Red Rum' 52
  'Scarlet Emperor' 52
  'White Lady' 52

S

safety, herbicides 82
sage 122
salad leaves 34, 60, 100
  see also lettuce
sandy soils 90, 92
sauces 147
Savoy cabbage 55
  'January King' 55
  'Tundra' 55
scabious 139

seating 25, 132–3
seaweed 94
security 141
sedums 122
seeds and seedlings 35, 37,
  38–9, 108, 111
  unusual cultivars 148–50
shade 19, 132–3
shallots 34, 38, 68
  'Eschalote Grise' 68
  'Golden Gourmet' 68
sheds 25, 141–3
shelter 132–3
Shirley poppies 140
shows 136, 159
shredders 102
Sibley, Will 12–13
silty soils 92
slow worms 129
slugs and snails 26, 39,
  125–6, 128, 140
soft fruit 41, 42
  see also different varieties
soils 28, 90–93, 110, 120
spinach 70, 100
  'Bloomsdale' 70
  'Galaxy' 70
  'Triathlon' 70
spraying 79, 82, 128
spring cabbage 54
  'Hispi' 54
  'Pixie' 54
spring greens 68
  'Mastergreen' 68
  'Wintergreen' 68
spring onions 34, 38, 69
  'Furio' 69
  'White Lisbon' 69
spring work programme 114
sprouting broccoli 32, 53
  'Early Purple Sprouting
    Improved' 53
  'Late Purple Sprouting' 53
  'White Eye' 53
squashes 70, 122
  'Baby Bear' 70
  'Squash Festival' 70
storing fruit and vegetables
  146–8, 151
strawberries 41, 69
  'Garigette' 69
  'Royal Sovereign' 69
succession planting 47
sugar snap peas, 'Sugar
  Crystal' 61
summer work programme
  115
sunflowers 137
supermarket produce 46
support 96–9, 133, 139

sweet corn 71, 95, 122
  'Earlisweet' 71
  'Indian Summer' 71
  'Swift' 71
sweet peas 138, 139, 140
sweet peppers
  'Big Banana' 64
  'Corno de Toro' 64
sweet Williams 122

T

targets 76–8
tayberries 61
thyme 122
time management 13, 87,
  106–7
tomato blight 129
tomatoes 72, 78, 149, 152–3
  storing 147, 148
  support 99
  'Black Russian' 72
  'Cherry Belle' 72
  'Costoluto Fiorentino' 72
  'Ferline' 121
  'Roma' 72
  'Santa' 72
  'Sungold' 72
  'Super Marmande' 72
  'Supersweet 100' 72
tools 28, 136, 141, 142–3
training 41–2
tulips 139, 140

W

waiting lists 18
wallflowers 138
water supply 19, 141
watering 94–5, 110, 152
weeds 19
  clearance 21, 78–85
  control 85–6, 110, 116
  seedlings 39
white rot 129
whitefly 122, 128
wildlife 140
winter moth 125
winter work programme 115

Y

yarrow 122

ACKNOWLEDGMENTS

The publishers are grateful to the following for
supplying photographs:

Paul Bullivant © The Royal Horticultural Society:
2–3, 4–5, 6, 20, 22, 29, 30–1, 38, 40, 41, 43, 44–5,
50, 52–3, 55, 56–7, 58, 59, 62–3, 64, 65, 70–1,
72–3, 77, 88–9, 91, 92, 97, 98, 101, 102, 103,
104–5, 108, 109, 123, 130–1, 135, 144–5, 148, 152
Alison Mundy © Royal Horticultural Society: 48–9
© Clay Perry: 10–11
© Royal Horticultural Society: 26–7, 54, 68–9
Tim Sandall © The Royal Horticultural Society:
14, 16, 33, 36, 42, 60–1, 66–7, 74–5, 82–3, 84,
112–3, 116–7, 118, 124–5, 127, 136
© Steven Wooster: 9, 80–1, 142–3, 154–5

Paul Bullivant thanks the following allotment
gardeners in Bristol for their assistance: Neil
Pirie, the Chairman and other members of the
Horfield and District Allotment Association
including Angela Morrison, Lorraine McGinn,
Mohamed and Fatima Naif, and Nalini Tondel;
and Stan Huckle, Secretary, Clive Bromhall,
Site Representative, and other members of the
Redland Green Allotment Association, including
Christina Hollow.